MW00978019

Cows In Church

80 Biblically Based Children's Sermons

B. Kathleen Fannin

Illustrations by Nancy Roberts

CSS Publishing Company, Inc., Lima, Ohio

COWS IN CHURCH

Copyright © 1999 by
CSS Publishing Company, Inc.
Lima, Ohio

Scripture quotations are from the *New Revised Standard Version of the Bible*, copyright 1989 by the Division of Christian Education of the National Council of the Churches of Christ in the USA. Used by permission.

Library of Congress Cataloging-in-Publication Data

Fannin, B. Kathleen.
   Cows in church : 80 biblically based children's sermons / B. Kathleen Fannin.
     p.   cm.
   ISBN 0-7880-1346-7 (pbk.)
   1. Children's sermons. 2. Church year sermons.   I. Title.
BV4315.F26   1999
252'.53—dc21

                                          98-33366
                                            CIP

This book is available in the following formats, listed by ISBN:
    0-7880-1346-7   Book
    0-7880-1347-5   Disk
    0-7880-1348-3   Sermon Prep

PRINTED IN U.S.A.

Acknowledgments

My heartfelt thanks to Phil Hoyle for giving me my first opportunities to present children's sermons; to Eddie Anderson and Moselle Smith for requesting a book of them; to Father Hugh Behan for discussions about them; to the children of First Christian Church in Jefferson City, Missouri, for their participation in them; to the many friends who have requested copies and provided feedback on them; to Karen Bartman for her many hours of prayerful support and encouragement and for critiquing the introduction; and to Nancy Roberts for the illustrations and her enduring faith that this book would happen.

B. Kathleen Fannin
Jefferson City, Missouri

Chesed

Table Of Contents

Introduction

"Let the little children come to me, and do not stop them; for it is to such as these that the kingdom of God belongs. Truly I tell you, whoever does not receive the kingdom of God as a little child will never enter it."   — Luke 18:16-17

————————

Children are a vital part of the church community. Though a full-length worship service may be too long to hold the attention of very young children, it is nonetheless important to include them for at least part of regular services. It is fundamental to them as young Christians to participate in this crucial aspect of Christian life; it is essential to the community's wholeness and its future to value and nurture children in this way.

One means of providing meaningful participation for children as part of their worship experience is the "children's sermon." By whatever name it is called, this portion of worship has been greeted with mixed emotions by nearly everyone involved, for a variety of reasons.

Many pastors shy away from this aspect of worship altogether because they feel they do not know how to talk with children or they don't feel they have the knack for "doing" children's sermons. This book is designed to help alleviate that fear, not only to provide its readers with ideas for presenting specific texts to children, but also to offer an underlying methodology — a way of experiencing scripture concretely and relating it to everyday objects and life-events through which the texts can be made comprehensible even to very young children.

A Few Words Of Advice

In June, 1990, when the associate pastor of my church asked me to present the children's sermon the following Sunday because he would be out of town, I was terrified. I couldn't believe I heard myself agreeing to do such a thing. What did I know about talking with children?

"Oh, just a few words of advice," he noted as he jotted down the lectionary texts for the coming week. "You'll have all ages. The best thing you can do is pick an age group and stick to it."

Those words helped me through a number of children's sermons in the months to follow, though with experience it has become easier to adapt the delivery of the message to the age of the children who show up. I have also found that when there is a wide age-range, it is better to focus on the younger folks. They are the ones whose attention spans are the shortest. If they are not interested, they will quickly become disruptive as they find other ways to entertain themselves.

A second bit of wisdom was offered by an eight-year-old when I was talking with his mother in the grocery store. I happened to mention to her that I had been asked to give the children's sermon on Sunday. "Oh!" her son interrupted. "Don't EVER do a children's sermon without a visual aid."

I took his advice to heart. Almost always I have some object to engage the children's attention and from which I work around to the message of the text. On those rare occasions on which I simply cannot come up with an object that helps illuminate the chosen scripture, I try to involve the children in other ways, including asking them questions or engaging them in physical activities.

Yet a third word to the wise comes out of my own experience in talking with children: be brutally honest. This may seem obvious. We expect honesty from children; we need to give them the same consideration.

Finally, children are concrete thinkers and take things very literally. It is important to keep this in mind when presenting ideas to them. Piaget and others suggest that the ability to think abstractly usually does not develop until adolescence.[1] Children learn intuitively from about age four to seven years; they are capable of concepts, but these are based on intuition rather than on reason. From seven to twelve, children can reason things out, but their thought processes are attached to empirical reality — that is, they think concretely.[2]

Involvement Is Critical

The children *must* be involved if you want to keep their attention. Soon after I started giving children's sermons, a couple of parents stopped me after worship and inquired, "Why do you ask the children so many questions?"

"To keep them involved," I replied. "To hold their interest; to hear what *they* think and what *they* have to say."

"But how do you *know* what they're going to say?"

"I don't."

"Well, then how in the world do you prepare your children's sermons? Wouldn't it be easier and safer just to tell them stuff? I mean, they could say ANYthing!"

They not only could, they *do*! So, how do I prepare? With a lot of thought and a great deal of prayerful listening. As for asking the children questions, those parents were right. It *would* be "safer" not to ask, particularly since children will tell you some surprising things sometimes. But, I never go into worship without reminding myself that whatever happens during the time with the children, God is in charge, not me. And sometimes God speaks "out of the mouths of babes." I *always* learn something when I talk with our youngsters. I think we all do when we take the time to listen.

For me, the whole approach involves a certain attitude. I feel you have to treat children as you would anyone else. They have minds; they have ideas; they have a lot of wisdom to offer if we give them an opportunity to express it.

For The Kids

Children's sermons need to be for the children. Usually the rest of the congregation gets something out of them too. (More than once I've had someone tell me, "I got a lot out of the children's sermon today; it's more on my level.") But primarily, this time is for the children.

It is a time to teach, to listen, to learn, to interact. It is definitely *not* a time to "put the youngsters on display" or to make jokes at their expense. Nothing will stifle children's participation faster than the threat of embarrassment.

11

As you read through the children's sermons which follow, you will note that even when an answer is incorrect I try to find some positive response so the child doesn't feel embarrassed or criticized. Put yourself in their shoes and consider what it must be like to answer questions, sometimes *difficult* questions, in front of an entire room full of ADULTS!

Be Patient

Give children time to answer your questions. Sometimes it's difficult, particularly if *you* are nervous, to let a question just hang in the air. In educational circles this is known as "wait time," an intentional delay between ending a question and expecting an answer.[3] "Wait time" gives children a chance to think — but it can be scary for the one waiting.

At times like these, I try to remind myself that God doesn't mind silence; I'm the one who is uncomfortable. If it becomes evident that the children are not going to respond, rather than providing an immediate answer, I will sometimes rephrase the question to be sure they understood.

While it is usually a good idea not to use complex language, at times one cannot avoid a "big" word. Don't be afraid to use them. If we "protect" children from "big" words, they will never learn to use them either. As long as the words we choose are employed in a context that allows the children to intuit their meaning, "big" words can be a plus.

But be sensitive to the children. Watch their facial expressions. You can tell fairly quickly if they are not grasping whatever it is you are trying to get across to them.

Off The Cuff

The concrete, literal nature of children's conceptualization should be evident in the conversations recorded in this book. I have written them down just the way they occurred (often surprising me as they happened). I soon learned that there was no point in writing them down beforehand. For one thing, children don't put up with being read to in this situation. Secondly, the children always come up with ideas I've not thought of or ways of looking at things I've not considered. Listening to the youngsters and coming up with new insights is part of the joy of "doing" children's sermons.

Also, giving them "off the cuff" rather than writing them down in advance maintains flexibility and open-ended potential. When I begin, I have a rough idea of the point of departure (usually either the scripture or the "visual aid"), and, in a general way, I know our destination. But if I write down all the points in between, I may miss an exciting detour. The shortest distance from the beginning to the final destination might be a straight line of thoughts written out in advance. But the most meaningful path is not necessarily the shortest or most direct.

Don't Be Afraid

"Easy for you to say," you may be thinking. Not really. Even after five and a half years, I still get nervous — even downright scared sometimes.

Dr. William Oglesby of Union Theological Seminary once told me that the entreaty not to be afraid occurs 365 times in the Bible — once for every day of the year. And it's good advice when it comes to talking with children...

* Don't be afraid to listen to what they have to say.

* Don't be afraid to go in unforeseen directions they might lead you.

* Don't be afraid to ask them questions.

* Don't be afraid to let go and trust God to get you where you need to be — even if it's not the destination *you* had in mind.

Children's sermons are a lot less intimidating for the person presenting them when that person can "go with the flow." One reason I wrote this book is to offer ideas and insights for doing just that. Some of the episodes recounted here are rather wild. There were times when I almost panicked (like the day I walked into worship and did not know until I read my name in the bulletin that it was my turn to present the children's sermon).

I only garner the courage to do these things by reminding myself that I am *not* in charge; God is. No matter how impossible a situation might appear, when I remember that I don't have to work it out alone, my mind is freed; words just come, making connections that often astound me. It is my hope that your experiences in talking with children will be equally full of joy, serendipity, wonder, and blissful surprise.

---

1. Caine, Renate Nummela, and Caine, Geoffrey, *Making Connections: Teaching and the Human Brain* (Menlo Park, CA: Addison-Wesley Publishing Co., 1994), p. 160.

2. Groome, Thomas H., *Christian Religious Education* (San Francisco: HarperSanFrancisco, 1980), p. 245.

3. *Ibid.*, p. 159.

Wings

"Once Jesus was asked by the Pharisees when the kingdom of God was coming, and he answered, 'The kingdom of God is not coming with things that can be observed; nor will they say, "Look, here it is!" or "There it is!" For, in fact, the kingdom of God is within you.' " — Luke 17:20-21

Theme: *Self-esteem; encouragement of others; faith; hope.*

Visual Aid: *A stained glass butterfly. Other possibilities include a picture of a butterfly and/or a caterpillar or an actual chrysalis or live caterpillar in a jar (preferably with a twig or two and some leaves or blades of grass).*

———

"Without a doubt, Julia was a caterpillar! She lived in a bright meadow at the edge of a dark forest. A clear stream meandered through the middle of the meadow. Sometimes Julia would crawl to the stream's edge and peer into the water at her caterpillar face. Sure enough, she looked just like all the other caterpillars. There could be no doubt: Julia *was* a caterpillar.

"Julia's very best friend was a caterpillar too. His name was Herman. They spent their days playing caterpillar games with their caterpillar friends and eating grass and leaves. Caterpillars have to eat a lot to grow big and strong.

"Julia liked the other caterpillars, and she especially liked Herman. But she didn't like herself very much. You see, Julia didn't want to be a caterpillar; Julia wanted to be a butterfly.

"Sometimes the other caterpillars teased her about that. But Herman never did. In fact, Herman actually believed that one day Julia *would* be a butterfly. Whenever Herman expressed that opinion, the other caterpillars teased him. Julia didn't believe Herman was right either, but she wished the others wouldn't tease him for saying what he thought.

15

"Herman, however, ignored their taunts. 'Herman thinks Julia's going to be a butterfly!' they'd chant in a singsong voice. 'Herman believes in dreams!' And, of course, Herman did. In fact, Herman was so sure that Julia would one day be a butterfly that sometimes, just for a moment or two, Julia actually believed it herself.

"One day Julia decided this whole matter deserved more thought. If Herman was so very certain, maybe, just maybe ...

"She decided she could concentrate better if she wrapped herself up in a leaf. But she didn't want to risk falling out. After all, once she started thinking, she just might forget to hold on. So, she spun a few silk threads around the outside of the leaf to hold herself in.

"Then Julia started thinking. She thought about Herman. She thought about the other caterpillars. She thought about herself. She was a caterpillar, and about the only thing she was really good at was eating. That wasn't much to be able to say about yourself. She wanted so badly to fly! But flying required wings and Julia didn't have any wings; she was just a caterpillar. 'If only I could be a butterfly,' she thought with a heavy sigh.

"Rolled snugly in her leaf, Julia thought and thought and thought. She thought for *ten whole days*! By the time she decided to come out of her leaf, she was feeling dizzy with hunger. But she had decided to like herself just for herself, not for how she looked or what she could do.

"As she struggled out one end of the rolled-up leaf, she noticed that she felt different, as though she had changed somehow. Her back especially felt strange, but she couldn't turn her head far enough around to see it. Hungry as she was, she just had to go look at herself in the stream before she found something to eat.

"Julia climbed down from the branch her leaf was attached to and stalked over to the silvery water. 'That's odd,' she thought. 'My legs seem longer than they used to be.' She assumed the funny feeling in her legs was from lying motionless in the leaf for ten days. But as she reached the stream's edge and peered at her reflection she could hardly believe her eyes! She wasn't looking at a caterpillar. She was looking at a butterfly! There was no doubt about it! Just as Herman had said she would, Julia had become a *butterfly!*" (At this point I show the children the stained glass butterfly I have brought along.)

"That's why her back had felt so different. She had grown wings! Slowly she spread them, admiring their beautiful bright colors. Being brand-new wings, they were still a bit wet; but spread in the sunlight, they soon dried.

"Suddenly Julia remembered how hungry she was, and as if she had known all her life how to use them, lifted her wings to catch the breeze. From the air she spotted a delicious-looking flower and swooped down, landing lightly on a delicate purple petal. She drank her fill of the flower's nectar. Then, her hunger satisfied, she took off again, realizing her dream really had come true. Julia had wings! Julia could fly! Julia was a butterfly!"

The children have listened with avid attention to this story. Now I suggest to them, "In some ways the church is rather like Julia's leaf and its members are sometimes like Julia, wanting to fly, but not having enough faith in themselves to try. The church is a place where we can discover possibilities, dare to dream dreams,

and find people who believe in us even when we don't believe in ourselves. The church is a place where we can be transformed from caterpillars into butterflies.

"Herman had complete faith in Julia. He loved her and encouraged her to believe in herself. And one day she found her wings. Whenever we love and encourage other people, it's as if we can see the butterfly inside of them; love and encouragement help the other people see themselves as beautiful. They might even feel so good about themselves they feel like they could fly!

"Everyone gets discouraged sometimes. But whenever that happens to you, maybe you'll remember this story and think about all the people who love you just as you are, the people who see the butterfly inside of you. And when you begin to believe in yourself, to see yourself as those who love you do, you just might feel as if you could fly — because you've discovered your wings!"

What **Is** *This?*

"In the evening quails came up and covered the camp; and in the morning there was a layer of dew around the camp. When the layer of dew lifted, there on the surface of the wilderness was a fine flaky substance, as fine as frost on the ground. When the Israelites saw it, they said to one another, 'What is it?' For they did not know what it was. Moses said to them, 'It is the bread that the LORD has given you to eat.' "   — Exodus 16:13-15

Theme: *God's providence.*

Visual Aid: *A bracelet made out of candy strung on elastic.*

———————

"I've been thinking about the word 'providence' all week. Have you ever heard that word before? Do you know what it means?" The children shake their heads to indicate this word is meaningless to them. I continue: " 'Providence' comes from the word 'provide,' and has to do with the goodness of God, God's providing, what we sometimes call God's benevolence. 'Providence' is an important word. I'd like you to try to remember it while I tell you a story.

"This story has to do with unexpected providence in the desert. Have any of you ever been in a desert?" Several of the children indicate they have been, so I ask, "What was it like? Were there many plants?"

"Hardly any," one child tells me.

"There was a LOT of sand!" another offers.

"What about water?" I ask them. "Do deserts get much rain?"

"No, they're very dry," several children assure me.

"So, deserts are dry, sandy places without many trees or other plants. There's a story in the Bible about Moses leading the Israelites out of Egypt, where they had been slaves, into the wilderness.

19

That wilderness was a desert. As you might imagine, their journey was filled with trouble.

"Their first problem was a lack of water. They walked for three days without finding any! But, finally they reached an oasis. That's what places in the desert that have water are called. This oasis was named Marah and the water there was so bitter the people couldn't drink it.

"Needless to say, the people complained. They were *not* happy! So, God told Moses to put a certain type of tree in the water to make the water sweet. Then the Israelites drank their fill.

"After a while, they moved on to an oasis called Elim. They rested there under the shade of the palm trees that were able to grow there because of the water. It must have been difficult for the people to think about going any farther, for the next part of their trip would take them into a desert named Sin. It was a barren and desolate wasteland.

"But, they couldn't stay at the oasis of Elim forever. So, eventually they continued their journey. The farther they went, the more they forgot about the difficulties they had had in Egypt. They forgot about all the hard work they'd had to do for the Pharaoh and how badly he had treated them. Instead, they remembered the food they'd had to eat there and the water they'd had to drink. They remembered the shade of Egypt's trees too. Many of the people began to think maybe Egypt hadn't been so bad after all.

"After about six weeks the people were getting pretty hungry because food was very scarce in the desert. So, they went to Moses and asked him if he had led them into the wilderness just so they could all die of hunger!

"Of course, Moses wouldn't do that. But he could tell the people were beginning to think they had made a big mistake in following him, so Moses asked God what to do.

"God said, 'I will give my people meat to eat in the evening and bread in the morning.' And God did! Migrating quails, worn out from flying so far into the desert, fell at the people's feet. This made them easy to catch, so the Israelites had the meat God had promised.

20

"But the people really didn't see how God was going to provide bread for them in the desert. That's why it's not too surprising that when God did, at first the people didn't recognize that what God had given them *was* bread.

"There was dew on the ground in the morning and when it dried, the people saw small round things lying around. 'What *is* this stuff?' they asked Moses.

"Moses told them it was the bread God had promised. But because it was not what they had expected, they hadn't recognized it. After Moses told them what it was, the Israelites gathered up the bread and ate it. It was white and tasted like honey. They called it manna.

"Sometimes God provides things for us that we don't recognize too. I was in the grocery store yesterday thinking about this story since it had to do with food. And, guess what? God provided me with an idea of something to help demonstrate the meaning of unpredictable providence! What do you suppose I brought that you aren't expecting? And where do you suppose it is since my hands are obviously empty?"

With wide-eyed wonder the children begin to look around, at my hands, my clothes. Maybe there's something in my pockets; maybe there is something behind me. Finally one discerning child lets out a surprised shriek.

"What do you see, Joe?" I ask him, barely able to control my laughter.

"Your bracelet," he nearly yells. "It's made of candy!"

"You have sharp eyes," I compliment him. "It *is* made of candy ... and what do you suppose I'm going to do with it?"

"Give it to US?" several children ask with mounting anticipation.

"Yes, I'm going to cut the string with these scissors and give each of you a piece of my 'bracelet.' You didn't expect this, did you? And because you didn't expect it, you didn't recognize it at first as something to eat, just like the Israelites didn't recognize the manna in the desert.

"Now, before you go let's think one more time about what we talked over today. In the desert the Israelites experienced God's goodness, God's unpredictable what? ... say it with me ...

"Providence!" some of the children manage.

"That's right, God's unpredictable providence. It's a big word that comes from 'provide.' God took care of the Israelites in the desert. And God will always take care of you too."

People And Pencils

"Then Peter came and said to him, 'Lord, if another member of the church sins against me, how often should I forgive? As many as seven times?' Jesus said to him, 'Not seven times, but, I tell you, seventy times seven.' "   — Matthew 18:21-22

Theme: *Forgiveness; differences; tolerance.*

Visual Aid: *A collection of pencils in all shapes, sizes, colors, and stages of wear. Also, a supply of brand-new pencils to give to the children at the end of our time together.*

"Suddenly it's September, which for many of us brings the beginning of school," I begin. "Are any of you starting or going back to school this week?" About half of the children indicate they are.

"Well, tomorrow is Monday. I guess that will be your first day."

Several children look surprised and tell me school doesn't start until Tuesday.

"Why is that?" I ask.

"Because Monday's a holiday," they answer.

"Oh?" I question. "What holiday is it?"

"It's Labor Day!" they reply.

"Labor Day ... Oh yes, that's the day we take off from work to celebrate work. I suppose the reason you get the day off is because your work right now is school.

"You know, whatever work we do is often made easier when we use tools. For example, what types of tools might a carpenter use?"

"A hammer!"

"Nails!"

"A saw!"

This is a question the children can sink their teeth into. I ask another.

"What tools might a painter use?"

"A brush!"

"Rags!"

Children often make the most interesting observations.

"What tools might a teacher use?" I continue.

"Chalk!"

"A ruler!"

"Many of you will be seeing your teachers on Tuesday, and you will be using tools yourself, won't you? What are some of the tools you use in school?"

"Crayons!"

"Pencils!"

"Paper!"

"Scissors!"

"Books!"

"You all have come up with some great ideas and the list could get even longer, but let's think about pencils for a minute. Pencils come in lots of different colors, don't they? I picked up a few of the pencils I had at home this morning and brought them with me. Just look at them! Why, besides their many colors, they come in all different shapes and sizes too. We have short ones, long ones, fat ones, skinny ones — yet they are all pencils. Some of them are wooden; some are mechanical. Some of them have erasers; on some the eraser has been worn off. Some of them have a point; others are dull or have had the point broken off. But in all this variety, all of them are still pencils.

"When the point is broken off we have to sharpen a pencil before we can write or draw with it, don't we? A pencil has to have a point in order for us to use it. And if we make a mistake, what do we use?"

The children's answer is immediate: "The eraser!"

"Yes, the eraser. So it helps if the pencil we are using has an eraser. If it doesn't and we make a mistake, we have to find another eraser before we can make a correction.

"You know, people are a lot like pencils. We come in lots of different colors, and all sorts of sizes and shapes — tall people, short people, fat people, skinny people, medium-sized people. But regardless of our color, our size, or our shape, all of us are still people.

"And just like pencils, sometimes people are not understood because they haven't 'sharpened their point.' Beating around the bush instead of speaking with one another directly is often about as successful as using a pencil without a lead.

"Now, what about mistakes? If we make a mistake with a pencil, we can usually find an eraser. But what about mistakes we make with people? Where is the 'eraser' in that situation?"

The children think about this, but no one has an answer.

"That's a tough question, isn't it?" I ask. "The answer lies in the teachings of Jesus, who taught us to love one another and to forgive one another, again, and again, and again. Sometimes we make the same mistake a number of times and need to be forgiven

many times for the same thing. And sometimes, where forgiveness is concerned, we are hardest on ourselves. Even though others forgive us, it's as if our own 'eraser' is all used up. That's when we need to remember that God loves us just as we are, even with our mistakes. And if God can love us just as we are, that's how we need to love ourselves and one another too.

"Now, I've got a pencil here to give each of you as you go back to your seats. These pencils don't have points yet. I'm leaving it up to you to see that they each get one. As you sharpen and use these pencils, perhaps you will remember what we talked about today. Perhaps you'll remember how much like pencils people are. You may make mistakes sometimes, but mistakes can be forgiven. Just remember that no matter how many 'erasers' you wear out or how often your point gets lost, no matter what color you are, how tall or short you are, how plump or skinny you are, that you are a wonderful, lovable person. You are children of God and God loves you. I do too."

Prayer And Bumblebees

"...we look not at what can be seen but at what cannot be seen; for what can be seen is temporary, but what cannot be seen is eternal." — 2 Corinthians 4:18

Theme: *Courage; prayer; listening.*

Visual Aid: *A church bulletin; a picture of a bumblebee, a stuffed animal bumblebee, or a puppet bumblebee.*

"Every week the hard-working folks in our church office put together a bulletin for our worship service. It gives us a guide to follow so we know what's coming next. It tells us the page numbers of the hymns, provides the words for the call to worship, the scripture, and the benediction. It tells us who is doing what, when, in the service. You can see, even if you can't read yet, that there's quite a list of things in the bulletin this morning. There's an anthem, a prelude, a postlude, the offering, communion, two sermons, four hymns, and SIX prayers! Wow! Six prayers! That's quite a lot compared to everything else, isn't it? That makes prayer look pretty important in the worship service, doesn't it?

"Prayer *is* important, you know. And not just during a worship service. Prayer is important every day in our lives. Jesus knew that. When we read about him in the Gospels we find he prayed both with other people and by himself. He went to the garden to pray (Mark 14:32); he went into the hills to pray (Matthew 14:23); he went to the wilderness to pray (Luke 5:16). Jesus talked with God a lot.

"When you talk with someone, especially if you ask a question, do you expect the other person to answer?" The children nod affirmatively.

"But unless you stop talking yourself, the other person won't be able to speak. You have to stop talking and listen if you are going to hear the other person's part of your conversation, don't you?" The children again nod their agreement.

"I think sometimes we forget that part of prayer needs to be listening too. If we do all the talking, how can God answer? Have you ever thought about that? Prayer isn't just talking to God; it is also listening to God.

"Sometimes, when it seems like a prayer is unanswered, it may be because we aren't listening. Or maybe we don't know how to listen. Maybe God is answering in a way we can't hear with our ears. Maybe we need to listen with our other senses. Have you ever listened with your eyes?" This suggestion elicits giggles from the assembled children.

"That may sound silly," I continue, "but I had an experience like that just last month. I was sitting at the edge of some woods listening for God. I had already done my talking. I had asked God to help me with something I had to do that seemed absolutely impossible. Now I was sitting there listening. The sun was setting and everything was quite still. Then suddenly two giant black and yellow bumblebees flew into the weeds in front of me.

"How many of you have ever seen a bumblebee?" I ask. Several children raise their hands. Others look uncertain, so I hold up the picture I have brought.

"This is what a bumblebee looks like," I tell them. The puzzled looks disappear from the uncertain children's faces.

"The bees I saw were almost as big as my thumb! As I watched them I remembered reading that from everything scientists know about flying, bees really shouldn't be able to fly. Their big round bodies are just too big to be lifted by their tiny little wings. But bees DO fly.

"You know, it surprised me to see these bees so late in the evening. There were no flowers around that part of the woods. In fact, the bees' presence didn't make any sense at all until I remembered why I was there. I had come to spend some time in prayer. And now it seemed as if God was using the bees to answer my prayer — if only I would listen.

"God wasn't taking any chances with me either. God sent two bees so I'd be sure to notice. But to get the message, I had to listen with my eyes.

"Probably you're wondering what that message was. The bees reminded me that supported by God's love, anything is possible. Even bees can fly!

"God speaks to us in many wonderful ways. But we can't hear if we don't listen. And sometimes we need to listen with something other than our ears. Sometimes it's important to listen with our eyes."

Least Coins

"For just as the body is one and has many members, and all the members of the one body, though many, are one body, so it is with Christ." — 1 Corinthians 12:12

Theme: *Discipleship; self-esteem; community.*

Visual Aid: *A jar of 100 pennies.*

"A few minutes ago you heard about a special part of the 'Festival of Sharing' called 'Least Coins — Terrific Trees.' It's a campaign aimed at collecting money to buy trees for reforesting areas in which lots of trees have been destroyed by fire, or earthquake, or other disaster. What type of money do you suppose is meant by 'least coins'?

"A dime?" a boy tentatively suggests.

"That's a good guess. A dime is the smallest coin we have as far as its size. However, there is another coin that is a little larger in size but it's worth only one-tenth as much as a dime. Does anyone know what that is?"

"A penny!" several children answer.

"Yes, a penny! Pennies are our coins of least worth. Last Sunday, when we were asked to bring pennies today, a comment was made about how quickly pennies seem to multiply in one's pocket or purse. So I decided to see what would happen during the week if I didn't take any pennies out of my pocket, but only put them in. Whenever I paid for something at the store, instead of getting pennies out to pay the exact amount, I just left them in my pocket, and added any other pennies I received in change. Last night, when I took out all the pennies I had gotten during the week, I had 48 of them!

"I spread them out on the table to count them. As I did, I noticed they all had dates on them, and some of them were shiny and new, while some of them were dark from use. The shiny ones had the most recent dates.

"As I looked at the darker ones, I thought about how they got that way — from being out in the world, passed from hand to hand, dropped on the ground, or stuffed in someone's pocket, alongside who knows what else, only to be found later by some mother at the bottom of her washing machine because a child or husband forgot to empty his pockets. Pennies *are* our least coins, and because of that, too often we are careless with them.

"But even pennies can be important. Since I had collected 48 pennies during the week, I went to my piggy bank to get 52 more. Do any of you have a piggy bank?"

"I do! I do!" one child eagerly replies.

"Is your bank shaped like a pig?"

"No, it's an army tank," he tells me. (One never knows what is going to come out of one of these conversations with children!)

"I see," I respond, trying to continue my thought as a part of my brain takes off pondering the pros and cons of giving a child a bank shaped like a tank. "Well, my bank is shaped like a pig and I got 52 more pennies out of it so I would have a total of 100. Here they are, in this jar. Now, who knows what 100 pennies is equal to?"

"A dollar!" the children reply in chorus. Money is one of those aspects of living with which they are very familiar.

"That's right," I proceed. "With 100 pennies, I have one dollar. But, if I take even one penny out of this jar, do I still have a dollar?" The children shake their heads negatively.

"No, I have only 99 cents in the jar after I take a penny out. Well, if I want to buy something that costs a whole dollar, can I buy it without this penny I took out of the jar?"

Again, the children shake their heads.

"No, I can't, can I? So this penny is very important, isn't it? You know, the church is sort of like that dollar. It's made up of many members and together we all form one group. But each of us is an individual part of the whole. Like the pennies that are part of the dollar, we are of different ages and colors, but even the least of us is an important part of the church. The church would be less without any one of us.

"But sometimes we treat ourselves or one another as we treat pennies. We may think someone doesn't particularly matter and fail to pay attention to him or her. Or we may get down on ourselves, think we aren't worth much, and decide maybe we won't come to church because no one is going to miss us if we don't show up.

"But that's not true. Every one of us, every one of *you*, is very important to this congregation. Just like the dollar, the church needs all of us — every one of its pennies — to be whole. Each penny we take away from the dollar lessens what it can buy; each member who takes himself or herself out of the church lessens what the church can do. So the next time someone hands you a penny in change, or you find one on the ground, you might think about how important it can be, even though it's our 'least coin.' And when you do, maybe you'll remember how important you are too."

Cows In Church

"And she gave birth to her firstborn son and wrapped him in bands of cloth, and laid him in a manger, because there was no place for them in the inn."   — Luke 2:7

Theme: *Advent; love; laughter.*

Visual Aid: *A wooden manger with hay in it.*

"We have some competition for our space on the chancel steps this morning. What is that thing?"

"A manger," one of the older boys announces eagerly.

"A manger?" I question. "I wonder if there is anything in it. Would one of you up there on the top step stand up and see?" One of the older children complies.

"There's hay inside," she reports.

"Well, that's about what I expected. You see, mangers were used in barns and stables to hold the hay for horses and cows so they wouldn't have to eat off the floor. Did any of you see any cows in church this morning?" My question elicits surprised laughter from the children.

"That seems like a silly question, doesn't it? Who ever heard of cows in church?! Well, I didn't see any here this morning either. I only asked because we have this manger with hay in it, apparently waiting for something — maybe waiting for the cows to come eat their dinner." This comment elicits more delighted grins; children know when they are being teased.

"But, you know better, don't you? You know the manger is here waiting for a very special baby whose birth we will celebrate on Christmas. Well, imagine for a moment that you are in Bethlehem on that night nearly 2,000 years ago when he was born. Imagine you are in the stable. You see Mary, Joseph, baby Jesus, shepherds, and animals.

33

"We've been talking about cows in church this morning, so I'd like for you to think in particular about a cow that might have been there, and assume that the cow eventually got hungry and went over to the manger to eat some hay. Can you imagine how very surprised it must have been to find a **BABY** sleeping in its dinner? It must have been as surprised as we would be to see cows in church! But God is like that, full of surprises. And Jesus is the best surprise God ever sent us.

"After Jesus was born, some wise men came and brought him gifts. What if you were in the stable with them now? What gift do every one of you have that you might offer this newborn child?"

"Caring!"

"Sharing!"

"Love!"

"Those are three very good ideas. And how might you show that love to a brand-new baby? How do you show love to one another? Do you think a hug would be a nice gift?"

"Oh, yes!" is the enthusiastic response from some of the children.

"I guess so ..." comes from some of the others.

"I think it would make a wonderful gift. And it's one you all have to give. But there is still one more present that you haven't guessed. It has to do with why I brought up something this morning so silly as cows in church. Did you ever think of laughter as a gift?"

Numerous little heads shake their negative answer.

"No? Well, it is. Laughter is something you can share with almost everyone, even with a perfect stranger. Laughter is something you can share with people of other cultures, other countries, the entire world. Laughter can be an expression of love, a gift you all have within you, a gift that is well worth giving.

"So, this week, when you give someone a hug or when a giggle bubbles up from deep inside you, remember what we talked about this morning. Remember the silliness of cows in church. Remember why the manger with the hay is really here. And know, as we await the coming of Jesus to the manger, that the gifts of love and laughter he brings can be yours every day — yours to receive, and yours to give away."

Lost And Found

"'Which one of you, having a hundred sheep and losing one of them, does not leave the ninety-nine in the wilderness and go after the one that is lost until he finds it?'" — Luke 15:4

Theme: *Separation from God; children of God.*

Visual Aid: *A cardboard box containing lost and found items (perhaps a sweater or cap, a pencil, a comb, and so forth).*

———————————

"How many of you have ever heard of a lost and found box, at your school or daycare center?" Several children raise their hands.

"Have any of you ever lost anything and then found it again?" Again, several children raise their hands. One of the more outspoken ones says, "I lost my blanket once; it took two days to find it!" I suspect there is an interesting story here, but rather than get into unknown territory I just tell him I'm glad he found it after it was lost.

"It's difficult to lose something you really care about, isn't it — especially if you don't ever find it again. When I was your age, the whole idea of a 'lost and found' box just didn't make any sense to me. Obviously if something was lost, it was lost; if something was found, it was found. How could something be both lost and found?

"Finally it dawned on me one day that in order to be found and get taken to the 'lost and found' box, an item first had to be lost by someone else. And since the person who lost it didn't know it had been found, it was still lost. Then the combination of 'lost and found' at last began to make sense.

"Have any of you ever gotten lost in a department store or a grocery store?" Once again, several hands go up. Acknowledging their responses with a nod, I continue.

36

"It's a frightening experience, isn't it? I used to be afraid that I might get lost like that when I was your age. I knew if I did, someone would eventually take me to the store's office. Then the store manager would use a microphone to ask in a loud voice, throughout the store, 'Would Kathleen's parents please come to the office. We have your child.' I did **NOT** want that to happen, so I was careful not to let my parents get away from me whenever we went shopping. Besides, if I did get lost and taken to the manager's office, what guarantee did I have that my parents would even know how to find the office? And if they couldn't find it, I'd *really* be stuck! It was better not to get lost in the first place.

"You know, sometimes people get lost from God, just like in the store. At first I thought, 'God doesn't have a lost and found box to look in. And God doesn't have a store manager either.' Can't you just hear the announcement? 'Would God please come to the office? We have your child.'

"However, I was talking with a friend the other day about these ideas and she said, 'But God **DOES** have store managers, lots of them!' She pointed out that every time any one of us knows of a friend who is hurting and feeling alone and we ask God in our prayers to be with that person, we are, in effect, doing the same thing the store manager would have done. We are saying, 'God, my friend is feeling lost and needing you right now. Won't you please come be with my friend?'

"Well, eventually I did get lost in a store — but it was only a couple of years ago." The children greet this confession with looks of surprise.

"That's right!" I assure them. "I was an adult! I had been shopping with my husband and we had gotten separated. I really didn't want to go to the manager and hear the announcement: 'Would Mr. Fannin please come to the office. We have your wife!'

"While I was looking for my husband, it occurred to me that he was probably looking for me too. Therefore, it would make more sense if I just stopped where I was and waited for him to find me. I did; he did.

"I think sometimes our relationship with God is like my experience in the store. Something catches our attention and we wander away; often we don't know how to find our way back. But we are all children of God, and we need to remember that God is searching for us just as we are searching for God. Sometimes all we have to do is stand still and stop looking long enough to be found."

Your Eyes Are Bigger Than Your Stomach!

"The LORD spoke to Moses and said, 'I have heard the complaining of the Israelites; say to them, "At twilight you shall eat meat, and in the morning you shall have your fill of bread; then you shall know that I am the LORD your God." ' "

"This is what the LORD has commanded: 'Gather as much of it as each of you needs.' "

"And Moses said to them, 'Let no one leave any of it over until morning.' But they did not listen to Moses; some left part of it until morning, and it bred worms and became foul. And Moses was angry with them." — Exodus 16:11-12, 16a, 19-20

Theme: *Trust; greed.*

Visual Aid: *Perhaps a menu or a loaf of bread. (I broke the "rules" on this one and didn't use a visual aid!)*

"What are some of the things we need to help our bodies grow?"

"Milk," one of the shyer boys softly announces from his seat at the edge of the gathered children.

"Vegetables!" a little girl says with an air of authority. The other children grimace at the thought.

"Sunshine!" says another, obviously beaming with joy that she came up with something important.

"Yes, we need all of those things, and more. Do all of you like to eat?" Most of the children nod affirmation, though some are obviously at an age still indifferent to food.

"Do any of you ever go out to eat?" All the children nod yes this time. "When I was a child, my parents took me out to eat once in a while. Quite often, especially if we went to a cafeteria, they would warn me, 'Be careful! Your eyes are bigger than your stomach.' Have any of you ever had anyone tell you that?" This time only two hands go up.

"A couple of you have. 'Your eyes are bigger than your stomach!' That expression just didn't make any sense to me when I was your age. I had seen drawings of the stomach on posters at my doctor's office. I knew it had to be at least as big as my fist. Both of my eyes put together weren't that big. 'What in the world could my parents mean?' I wondered. But as I got older and continued to hear it, I learned that my eyes could see more than my stomach could hold. My parents wanted me to be careful not to take more food than I could eat. Finally I understood what it meant to have eyes bigger than my stomach.

"In a few minutes our Liturgist is going to read a story about the Israelites wandering in the wilderness. They got pretty hungry and were upset with Moses for leading them to a place with so little food. So Moses asked God what to do. God said, 'I'll feed them, but they must gather only as much food as they need for one day and not leave any of it for the next day.'

"That was hard for some of the Israelites to do. They had been very hungry. When God provided food, some of them gathered up more than they needed and tried to save it. But the extra food spoiled by the second day and they couldn't eat it. If they had obeyed God and only gathered enough for one day, they wouldn't have wasted the extra food they had taken.

"Sometimes it's hard not to take more than we need, isn't it? Sometimes it's hard to trust that something will be there tomorrow if we don't take it today. But that's what God asked the Israelites to do.

"Sometimes we're so hungry when we sit down to supper or go out to eat that it's extra hard not to take more than we need; it's hard not to have eyes bigger than our stomachs. Yet when we do, the food that is left over sometimes gets thrown away or sits in the refrigerator too long and spoils. That's rather sad when there are people all over the world who don't have enough to eat. In fact, there are people right here in Jefferson City who don't have enough to eat. That's why the church has a food closet, isn't it?

"Well, in about an hour many of you will be sitting down to your Sunday dinner. When you do, you might think about what we've talked about this morning and try to take only what you need. In fact, whenever you eat, you might think about not having eyes too big for your stomach, and having faith that you can have more another time. You might think about how God asked the Israelites to have faith, to trust God. You know, God needs your trust too."

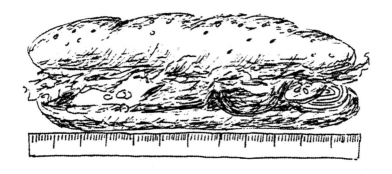

41

"Remember Me!"

"Now on that same day two of them were going to a village called Emmaus, about seven miles from Jerusalem, and talking with each other about all these things that had happened. While they were talking and discussing, Jesus himself came near and went with them, but their eyes were kept from recognizing him. And he said to them, 'What are you discussing with each other while you walk along?' "

— Luke 24:13-17

Theme: *Friendship; communion.*

Visual Aid: *I did not use one; a picture of a dog, cat, or some other animal which might be a pet would work.*

"Raise your hand if you have a pet!" Immediately almost every child present shoots an arm into the air.

"What kind of pet do you have?" I ask a boy in the front row.

"A cat!" he answers with an air of authority, almost as if he'd add, "What else is there?" if he were a few years older. This tries the patience of the other children. Immediately the sanctuary is filled with their eager young voices:

"I have a cat too!"

"We have a dog!"

"I have a cat AND a dog!"

"I have a turtle!"

Above this melodious cacophony I hear the plaintive wail of a little girl seated on the middle of the top chancel step: "I don't have a pet."

"If you had a pet," I inquire of her, "what would you like it to be?"

"I don't know," she says.

"Have any of you ever lost a pet?" I ask the group. Hands go up. Heads nod affirmation as some of the older children recall pets of their younger years. "How did you feel when that happened?" I ask.

"Pretty bad," says one boy.

"Awful!" sighs another.

"Afraid ..."

"Alone ..."

"Hurt ..."

I want the children to remember their feelings and share them, but at the same time I do not want them to dwell on such feelings too long, so I change the subject.

"I need another show of hands," I announce. "How many of you have a 'best' friend?"

As a number of children raise their hands, from the back row I again hear the plaintive voice of the little girl who doesn't have a pet.

"I don't have a best friend," she pouts.

"Do you have a good friend?" I question.

"No," she responds looking downcast, "I don't have any friends."

I find myself wondering if this child is really friendless, or if she's learned that a negative response to her world is what gets her attention (in which case she might indeed be friendless). At the last moment she gives me a reprieve.

"I do have some cousins, though," she states in a brighter voice. Inwardly I heave a sigh of relief as I move on to my next question.

"How many of you have ever had a very good friend move away to another city?" A few hands go up.

"How many of you have moved yourselves and had to leave good friends behind?" More hands go up.

"How did you feel when you were separated from your friends?"

"Pretty bad," says one boy.

"Awful!" sighs another.

"Afraid ..."

"Alone ..."

"Hurt ..."

"Do any of you ever write to those friends?"

43

Some heads nod yes. One young lady says, "I haven't yet, but I'm going to." I recall that she and her family have only recently moved into our community. One boy is emphatically shaking his head.

"You haven't written to your friend?" I question.

"Not ever," he responds.

"But you still remember your friend?"

"Oh yes!" he nearly shouts, and his face suddenly lights up as he obviously thinks of times past shared with his friend.

"I've asked you to recall these feelings because it's only been a couple of weeks since Easter. What happened to Jesus on the Friday before Easter?"

"He was crucified," replies one of the older girls with a note of sadness.

"How do you suppose the disciples felt when Jesus died?" I continue.

"Pretty bad..."

"Afraid ..."

"Awful ..."

"Alone ..."

"Hurt ..."

"Yes, I expect they felt all of those things, and maybe just a little bit angry too. Because Jesus had been their teacher, their leader, their best friend — and now he was dead!

"But Jesus came back didn't he?" Heads with dancing curls and freshly shorn locks bob eagerly up and down. "How do you suppose the disciples felt when Jesus came back?"

"Wonderful!"

"Happy!"

"Like jumping up and down!"

"Maybe surprised," offers one insightful child.

"Well, I expect they felt all of those things and more. When Jesus was with the disciples, he taught them many things. And when he knew the time was growing near for him to leave them, he said to them, 'Remember me!'

" 'Remember me ...' Of all the things Jesus said, that is the thought which has been on my mind this past week. We have many things to help us remember him. We have many stories in the Bible, both stories he told and stories told about him. We have the community of the church. And, when you get just a bit older, you will remember Jesus as you take communion.

"There is one other way in which we remember him too: through one another. Every time we do something kind for someone else, every time we remember a friend with a letter or a phone call, every time we offer someone a hug, or an encouraging word, or in some other way show our love, we are remembering Jesus. That's what I'd like you to think about this week. And the next time a friend leaves or a pet dies and you feel afraid, lost, alone, or hurt, maybe you won't feel quite so alone or quite so lost because each of you has a very special friend who is with you always. His name is Jesus. All you need to do is remember ..."

Tall Enough

*"I lift up my eyes to the hills — from where will my help come?
My help comes from the LORD, who made heaven and earth."*
— Psalm 121:1-2

Theme: *Needing help.*

Visual Aid: *A small stepladder.*

"Is anyone here this morning who is eight years old?" One young lady, somewhat shyly, holds up her hand. "Ah, I see one of you is. When I was the age of most of the rest of you (younger than eight), I had two great goals in life. The first was that I wanted to be eight years old. The second was that I wanted to be tall enough to see the top of the refrigerator. I knew if I could just wait long enough and if I ate all my vegetables, I'd BE eight one day AND I'd be tall enough to see the top of the refrigerator too." A few of the children make faces as I speak of eating vegetables.

"I tried to be patient, but sometimes the waiting got hard. In fact, sometimes when people asked me how old I was, I said, 'Eight!' even though I wasn't yet. Sometimes it seemed like saying I was eight would make it true sooner.

"Then one day in February, many, many years ago, I woke up to my eighth birthday. It was wonderful actually to have a dream come true, especially since we had moved recently...

"You see, we lived in a rented house, and when we moved, that refrigerator I was so sure I'd get tall enough to see the top of stayed behind. The refrigerator in the new place was TALLER than the old one. That meant I was going to have to wait longer and grow some more to be tall enough to see the top of the new one.

"But finally the day came that I knew I was getting close. I couldn't see it yet, but I could touch the top of the refrigerator with my hand. I just had to wait a little longer ...

"About then, we moved *again*. And guess what?"

"You got another refrigerator with the new house and it was taller!" several of the children say together.

"That's right!" I respond. "And, do you know what else?" The children look puzzled, obviously trying to think what else there could be.

"I never have grown tall enough to see the top of our refrigerator — at least, not without help. We moved a lot and went through quite a few refrigerators before I realized all I had to do to see the top of it was to stand on something, something like this stepladder I am sitting on.

"This is a very OLD ladder. In fact, it was right in front of me all those years when I thought I wasn't tall enough to see the goal I had set for myself. Help was right there, right in front of me. However, because I thought I needed to 'do it on my own,' I didn't see the ladder.

"But one day, I could stand the suspense no longer; I finally used the ladder. There really wasn't much to see on top of the refrigerator, but I learned something important from the experience. I learned that it's all right to need help sometimes; I learned that sometimes help is right in front of us and we just don't see it; and I learned that it's all right to ask for help. In fact, sometimes when we ask for help, we are telling another person 'I need you.' Sometimes, it's nice to know you're needed.

"No matter how tall you get or how long you live, there will always be times when you need help. And there will always be someone you can ask for help. Who do you suppose I mean?"

"Jesus?" says one child with a question mark in her voice.

"Yes, Jesus, your friend who is always there no matter what. Some of you may not ever grow tall enough to see the top of your refrigerator, at least, not without standing on a ladder. But I do hope you'll remember that it is all right to ask for help; it's all right to ask another person for help and it's all right to ask God too. God listens to our prayers, you know, and answers them, even though we may not recognize the answer or the answer may be 'No.'

"And just as we ask things of God, sometimes God asks things of us. But of one thing you can be sure: God is never going to ask you to reach higher or farther than your arms will stretch. So if it ever seems like God is asking you to reach an 'impossible' goal, you might remember to look around for the help God is surely offering at the same time. Like this ladder, it may be right in front of you!"

Living Water

"Jesus answered her, 'If you knew the gift of God and who it is that is saying to you, "Give me a drink," you would have asked him, and he would have given you living water.' " — John 4:10

Theme: *Prayer; spirit.*

Visual Aid: *A small potted cactus. (An unusual pot will elicit more interest from the children.)*

_____

As the children gather on the steps they see I am holding a small cactus planted in a pot shaped like a cat. "What did I bring with me this morning?" I ask them.

"A plant in a cat!" some of them respond.

"Yes, a cactus in a cat," I tell them. "What does this cactus need to live in this pot?"

"Sunshine!" says one little boy.

"Yes, it needs sunshine. What else does it need?"

"Water," replies a little girl.

"Yes, it needs water. And there is something else it needs." I start to tilt the pot to the side as I speak. "What are its roots in? What is holding it in the pot?"

"Dirt!" most of them say triumphantly.

"That's right, dirt. The cactus gets food from the dirt.

"Well, what I have to say to you this morning may be one of the most important things I ever tell you. But, it's a little hard to understand. That's why I brought this plant along, to help me explain it to you. Like the cactus, all of you need sunshine, water, and food to live, though you don't *eat* dirt — at least not usually!"

"You need all of these things for your physical health and to give you the energy to use your mind. But your spirit needs something too. Perhaps this will be easier to understand if you think of your spirit as a plant inside you — probably not a prickly one like

49

this cactus; you wouldn't want to be all prickly inside!" Several children shake their heads in agreement, grinning.

"Now this spirit, this plant inside you needs a special kind of 'water' to live — it's something Jesus called 'living water.' It isn't like the water from the rain, or the water several blocks from here that flows in the Missouri River. It isn't like the water you get out of a faucet. You can't see it, or touch it, or taste it, but you can feel it, at times of great joy or sadness, and at very quiet times. It is the feeling that brings tears, which you could think of as 'rain,' and laughter, which you could think of as the rainbow that follows the rain. It is spirit 'stuff' and it comes to us from God, through God's son, Jesus. And the only way to get it is to ask. That means it is important to take time to pray, quiet time, to talk with God and listen to God so that we can receive this 'water' for our spirits.

"Tonight when you go to bed, before you go to sleep, you might whisper a prayer, asking God for this invisible 'living water' of the spirit. You might think of your spirit as a little plant inside you that is thirsty, and ask God to give it a drink."

Masks

"Now the Lord is the Spirit, and where the Spirit of the Lord is, there is freedom. And all of us, with unveiled faces, seeing the glory of the Lord as though reflected in a mirror, are being trans-formed into the same image from one degree of glory to another."
— 2 Corinthians 3:17-18

Theme: *Being yourself; friendship; self-esteem.*

Visual Aid: *A bandanna large enough to wear as a mask.*

"Good morning, children! Some of you are laughing. Why is that?"

"Because you're wearing a handkerchief on your face!" says one little girl as the others giggle.

"Because I'm wearing a handkerchief on my face ... Is that funny?" Several of them nod. "Haven't you ever worn a handker-chief?" I ask them.

"Well, yes," one child replies, "but **NOT** on my face!"

"Not on your face?!" I say in mock surprise. They giggle again. "This handkerchief is like a mask, isn't it? It's hiding part of my face." The children nod, obviously waiting to see what silly thing I'm going to do next.

"Well, why would I need to wear a mask with all of you?" I ask.

"You *don't!*" a couple of children reply emphatically.

"You are absolutely right," I agree with them. "I don't need a mask with you, because I know all of you and you are my friends." As I say these words, I pull the bandanna down from my face to let it hang around my neck.

"You know, sometimes in life we feel that we do need a mask to hide behind or a hole to crawl into. Sometimes we get embar-rassed by saying something in a way we didn't mean or doing something that makes us feel silly. Sometimes we are afraid of something and would like a mask to hide behind. But what several of you said just a minute ago is very true — you don't need a mask with your friends.

"Friends are folks who accept us without masks. But, if we go around wearing a mask, how is anyone going to know who we really are?

"There is one friend that all of us share in common. This isn't a friend we can see like I can see you and you can see me; but this is a friend, nevertheless, who loves us unconditionally. Do you know who I mean?

One child points upward with a shy grin. "Who are you pointing to?" I ask.

"God...?" she says with a slight question and a big sigh.[1]

"Yes," I answer, "God, a friend who is always with you even when it seems like you are all alone. Each of you is a child of God, created to be just who God would have you be. When we put on a mask, that is, when we act in a way that is not truly how we feel or think, then we are not being ourselves. If we go through life that way, we even risk forgetting who we really are; we may start to believe the 'mask' is the real us, and so does everyone else since our false face is the only one we ever let anyone else see.

"Well, the thought I would leave you with this week is that it is important to be yourself; it is important not to go through life with a mask; it is important to be who God made you to be. So this week, whatever you do, dare to be yourself. God loves you because you are who you are. So do the rest of your friends who get to see the real you, without any masks."

----

1. One must be prepared to respond to whatever answer the children give. If this little girl had said, "Jesus," the same point could be made in a slightly different way. If she had said, "Our parents," it would be wise to agree with her and then to ask about another friend to whom we can turn.

"Invisible" Milk

"Do you see someone who is hasty in speech? There is more hope for a fool than for anyone like that." — Proverbs 29:20

Theme: *Don't act in haste.*

Visual Aid: *An opaque drinking glass.*

"I have a story to tell you this morning about something that happened when I was five. Is anyone here this morning five years old?" Several children raise their hands. I direct my next question to them.

"Do you have trouble seeing what is on the table when you sit in your chair at mealtimes?" Their little faces look very serious as they bob their heads up and down indicating they do.

"I did too, when I was your age. One evening I sat down at the dinner table with my family. As I looked around to see what we were having for dinner, I noticed I didn't seem to have any milk in my glass. We didn't use glasses made from glass back then. The glasses we had were like this one, made out of colored metal." I hold the metal glass out for everyone to see.

"From where I sat at the table that day, my glass looked quite empty. As you can see for yourselves, this glass is metal so you can't see through it. From where you all are sitting, you can't tell if there is anything in the glass or not. And that's how it was for me that day when I sat down to have dinner with my family.

"If I had been polite, I would have asked my mom or my dad if I could please have some milk. But I wasn't very polite and I wasn't very patient. So, instead of asking, I grabbed my glass and turned it upside down as I loudly announced, 'Hey! I didn't get any ...' I was going to say I didn't get any milk. But I never got to the word 'milk.' As I tell this portion of my story, I turn the glass

I have been holding upside down, to demonstrate what I had done that day.

"You see, there *had* been milk in my glass. But the glass wasn't as full as usual. So, sitting in my chair, I couldn't see the milk that was in it. Because I couldn't see any milk, I assumed it wasn't there. Because I assumed it wasn't there, I grabbed the glass and turned it over to point out the 'truth' of the words I was saying rather loudly, 'Hey! I didn't get any ...' But, of course, I had gotten milk. And because I had taken the action I did, there was now milk all over the table! Needless to say, I have never forgotten that day!

"Did your parents get mad?" one child inquires.

"I'm sure they were probably angry," I respond. "But, it is interesting that I really don't remember their anger. What I do remember is how foolish and bad I felt. *Much* to my surprise (because I really had thought the glass was empty), I had made a terrible mess. That was a very long time ago, yet I can still see that milk pouring out of that upside-down glass if I close my eyes and think about it! And I can still remember how awful I felt about what I had done.

"But I learned from my experience. I learned that I should never assume my glass is empty. It may be full if I will only take a closer look.

"You know, life is a lot like that glass. It can seem empty sometimes. But if we just take a closer look, we may find that life is really very full. Sometimes how we look at life makes all the difference. So, it's probably a good idea not to turn things upside-down until we take a second look."

Leaping On The Laundry

*"Be strong and courageous; do not be frightened or dismayed,
for the LORD your God is with you wherever you go."*
— Joshua 1:9

Theme: *Courage; self-reliance; Mother's Day*

Visual Aid: *A photograph of a cat nestled in a pile of laundry.*

"Is today a special day for someone in your family?" Heads
nod eagerly; faces light up with knowing smiles.

"What is today?"

"It's Mother's Day!" comes the boisterous, unanimous response.

"Yes, it's Mother's Day, a day to remember our mothers in
special ways."

I reach into my pocket for a picture I have brought to share and
hand it to the nearest child. "The individual in this picture reminded me of my mother a few weeks ago. You all can pass it
around so every one can see it while I tell you a story about him.
He's not a person, is he?"

"No!" say those who have seen it. "He's a cat!"

"That's right. He's a cat. His name is Roy. What is he doing
in this picture?"

"Sitting on a pile of laundry or something," one little girl responds.

"That's right; he's sitting on the laundry. Now Roy really likes
to sit on the back of the sofa in the rear bedroom of our house. A
few weeks ago, I was sitting on the seat of the sofa (I don't fit too
well on the back) while I put my shoes on. The night before, I had
brought two boxes of laundry upstairs from the basement, but I
hadn't folded any of it or put it away. Instead, I had set the boxes
of clothes on the back of the sofa — in Roy's favorite napping
place.

55

"Roy came into the bedroom as I was tying my shoelaces. He crouched down, preparing to jump up to the back of the sofa. Then, suddenly, he froze! There was SOMETHING in the way! He looked over at me and said, 'MEOW!' in his biggest voice. He seemed to be saying, 'Either move the clothes or help me up!'

"I watched him while I finished tying my shoes. Like most cats, he does not have much patience. 'MEOW!' he said again. I took that to mean, 'Do something, right now!'

"I got up to help him. But, just as I was bending over to pick him up, I thought, 'If I help him, he will never know that he could have done it by himself. If I just stand here behind him, so he knows I will catch him if he falls, and give him some encouragement, maybe he'll go ahead.'

"So, I stood behind him and told him he really could do it if he'd just try. He looked back over his shoulder at me one more time, said, 'Mew?' as if to make sure I meant it, then with a graceful leap, soared into the air and landed gently on the laundry where he made himself quite comfortable, as you can see from the picture. "Roy started purring (he was VERY pleased with himself) and I started thinking about what had just happened. It made me

56

think of all the times my mom (and my dad too) had encouraged me when I was afraid to do something. Whatever I was afraid of, they didn't do for me, but they stood behind me and encouraged me. They let me know they were behind me. I knew if I stumbled, they'd be there to pick me up. I knew if I fell, they'd be there to catch me. I even knew if I tried and failed, they would still love me and would encourage me to try again.

"You know, God is like that too. Sometimes when we pray we ask God to do things for us. But there are things which God must not do because we need to know we can do them for ourselves. Like my parents and yours, even if we try to do something and fail, God still loves us, just as we are. And, like our parents, God will keep encouraging us to try again."

Rainbows

"I have set my bow in the clouds, and it shall be a sign of the covenant between me and the earth." — Genesis 9:13

Theme: *Covenant; God's care.*

Visual Aid: *Ribbons tied into bows.*

"This morning I need all of you to help me understand a verse of scripture. It's from the ninth chapter of Genesis, verse 13." I read the verse to the children.

When God said to Noah, "I have set my bow in the clouds," what kind of 'bow' did God mean? Was it the kind of bow you shoot arrows with?" The eight girls and one small boy seated on the chancel steps grin at my silliness and shake their heads to indicate no.

"Was it the kind of bow some folks wear in their hair, like these?" I point to the pink ribbons I've tied to the ends of my braids for this discussion. Again the heads shake no, while some of the children say, "No!" with a giggle attached.

"Was it the kind of bow Stephanie has tied in her shoelaces?" The children now eye Stephanie's feet, then assure me it wasn't that kind of bow either.

"No? You all keep saying, 'No!' Well, then, what kind of bow was it?"

"A rainbow!" says one little girl triumphantly.

"Why did God set a rainbow in the clouds? I'll give you a hint — it was after forty days and nights of rain."

"To let Noah know the rain had stopped?" one of the children states with a question in her voice.

"Yes, and to let Noah know that never again would God destroy everything on the earth with a flood. The rainbow was the sign of an agreement between God and all of creation, a sign that said, 'I will remember my agreement with you whenever the rainbow appears in the clouds, because I love you.'

"It rained on Friday. Did anyone see a rainbow that day? No? Why not? Did the sun ever come out on Friday?"

Several children shake their heads indicating a negative response.

"The sun never came out on Friday. The sky was cloudy all day, from before the sun came up until after the sun went down. Does that give you a hint about why there were no rainbows?"

"Because there was no sun?" comes a tentative, questioning response.

"Right, because there was no sun! We have to have sunlight in order to have rainbows.

"Do any of you know what clouds are made of?" I ask with an abrupt change of direction.

"Rain!" says one of the children emphatically.

"Yes," I agree, "clouds are made up of little drops of water. And when the sunlight shines though them what do we get?"

"A rainbow!" several of the children declare.

"That's right. Now, who made the sun, and the clouds, and the rain, and all of creation?"

"God did," they answer.

"So, if we have to have sunlight and droplets of water to make rainbows and God made the sun and the rain, I guess it must be God who makes rainbows, just as we read in the verse from Genesis. Now, once again, what is the rainbow a sign of?"

"God's agreement with Noah?"

"Yes, but not just with Noah. It's a sign of God's agreement or covenant with every living creature on the earth. It's a sign God made to remind all of us that never again would God destroy everything with a flood. And it is one of the many ways God has of saying, 'I made you and I love you.' "

Gifts Of Love

*"For God so loved the world that he gave his only Son, so that
everyone who believes in him may not perish but may have eternal
life."* — John 3:16

Theme: *Love; giving; school.*

Visual Aid: *An apple.*

"What happened in some of your lives this week that hasn't
happened all summer?"

"We went to school!" the older children respond.

"Ah, yes, school has begun. Well, I have something in my
pocket that could have something to do with school. Whatever it
is, it's making *quite* a lump, isn't it?" The children nod affirmatively, some serious, some grinning as their imaginations spill over
onto their faces. "What do you think I have in my pocket to make
such a lump?"

"A ball?" one little girl asks.

"No, it's not a ball, but that's a good guess. You can see it's
sort of round."

"An apple!" states a boy in the center, with no trace of
uncertainty.

"Yes, it's an apple. Why do you suppose I would have an
apple in my pocket?"

"To eat it!"

"That's one thing I might do."

"To give it to your teacher!"

"Yes, that's another thing I might do with it. Why would I
give an apple to my teacher?"

"So she'd have an apple."

My personal public-speaking panic level begins to rise with that response. But I move on, asking, "Why would I want my teacher to have my apple?"

"So she could eat it!"

This conversation was getting nowhere fast; it was time to try another tactic. "You know, I gave several of my teachers apples when I was in school; so did some of my classmates. But I never once saw a teacher EAT an apple. Do teachers eat apples?"

"Of course they do!" several children reply all at once amidst the giggles of others.

"Well, then, that brings us back to why I would give a teacher an apple."

"Maybe because you liked her?" one child offered.

"Yes," I said, "maybe because I liked her — or even because I loved her. It *is* possible to love teachers ... if they're nice." This comment elicits several more giggles.

"Well," I continue, "almost 2,000 years ago, God gave us a very precious gift. Does anyone know what that was? I'll give you a hint: it wasn't an apple."

The children sit with puzzled looks on their faces, thinking about what God's gift might have been so long ago. As the silence grows, I prod their thoughts: "Two thousand years is a long time, isn't it? What did God give us so long ago? I'll give you another hint. God's gift was a person."

Immediately their faces light up with understanding. "Jesus!" several children exclaim together.

"Yes, God gave us Jesus, God's son. Why would God do that?"

"Because God loves us?" one of the older boys questions.

"That's right, because God loves us. You know, gifts are a wonderful way to tell someone you love him, and sometimes the nicest gifts are the ones we don't expect. When you surprise your teacher with an apple or give a friend a present just because the person is your friend, you're saying, 'You are important to me; I care about you.' And when people receive your gifts, they feel your love; through your love, they can know God's love too."

A little girl raises her hand. I nod to her and she says, "I gave my teacher some flowers this week."

"How nice of you!" I answer. "What are some of the other things, besides apples and flowers, you might give to your teachers?"

"A letter!"

"A banana!"

"A hug!"

"Yes! All of those are good presents. Sometimes something as simple as a smile is a wonderful present for a teacher. I hope you'll remember what we talked about this week: whenever you give a teacher, a friend, a brother, a sister, or anyone else a present because you love them, perhaps they will know that God loves them too — just as God loves each of you."

Cats, And Mice, And Mercy

"Blessed are the merciful, for they shall obtain mercy."
— Matthew 5:7

Theme: *Mercy; grace.*

Visual Aid: *A stuffed toy cat and a catnip mouse.*

———————————

Before I have even said, "Good morning," to the gathered children, one of the younger ones (who is anything but shy) asks, "Know what?" Wondering where it will lead, I answer, leaning on my faith that God is in charge of this process, and this time IS for the children. "What?" I respond.

"I'm MAD at my grandmother," the little girl announces. "She left my blanket at her house, and I'm cold!" This statement ends with a decidedly protruding lower lip, almost a silent challenge.

"That's too bad," I reply, "but I don't think your grandmother left the blanket on purpose. In fact, I bet right now she wishes as much as you do that you had your blanket." The little girl looks doubtful.

"Perhaps what happened to you this morning can help us understand the word 'mercy.' We've been talking about the Beatitudes the last few weeks. In one of them, Jesus said, 'Blessed are the merciful, for they shall obtain mercy.' Does anyone know what mercy means?"

One of the older boys suggests, "It's like when you're playing with someone, but you're not as hard on them as you could be; you don't beat them really bad."

"Are you saying that you're nicer or kinder than you could be or than they might expect?" I question. The young man agrees.

"That's a good example of mercy," I tell the group. "I've brought something this morning to help us try to understand mercy

64

better." With these words, I hold up a catnip mouse and ask the children, "What is this?"

"A mouse!" the kids practically shout.

"Is it a real mouse?" I ask, teasing them just a little.

"No!" they assure me.

"Well, I've brought something else for our discussion. What's this?" I ask, holding up a small stuffed animal.

"A kitty cat!" the children respond with obvious delight.

"It's a kitty cat," I agree. "And what do kitty cats do to mice?" I ask.

"Catch them!"

"Eat them!"

"Kill them!"

Their responses vary, but all the youngsters seem to have a definite idea of a mouse's fate with a cat.

"But they don't eat the bones," comes an afterthought from the child who is angry with her grandmother. By this time I am holding the stuffed cat's front paws together with the catnip mouse clutched between them.

"What do you suppose would be the merciful thing for this cat to do?" I ask.

"Let the mouse go!" the children answer.[1]

"Have you ever seen a cat do that?" I continue. This elicits laughter (and not just from the children) as the children give me a vehement, "No!"

"You don't expect a cat to let a mouse go free. But that's the nature of mercy; it's an unexpected kindness. Mercy can mean kindness, forgiveness, or, as Andrew suggested, not being as hard on someone as you could be. Mercy is the sort of kindness that comes as a surprise because the one who receives it really doesn't expect it. Jesus said, 'Blessed are the merciful, for they shall obtain mercy.' "

I turn my attention back to the little girl who is angry with her grandmother. "Brittany, I think a kindness your grandmother doesn't expect is that you would tell her, 'Grandmother, I know you didn't mean to leave my blanket at home, and I love you.' If you can let go of your anger and tell her that, you will be showing mercy.

"You know, that's how God is," I continue to the group as a whole. "When we mess up, when we do something that's wrong, God is merciful; God is forgiving. God is like that because God loves us, even when we make mistakes, just because we ARE; just because God made us.

"Let's pray together before we go: God, thank you for these children and the understanding they bring us in sharing faith with them and through them. Let us be merciful in our lives as we live them together, following the paths of kindness that lead us toward your love, the love you have shown us with the greatest mercy of all in the gift of your Son, Jesus Christ. It is in his name that we pray. Amen."

---

1. I later learned of an adult's response to this question: "Eat it quick!"

Differences

Theme: *Differences; tolerance.*

Visual Aid: *Lilacs in three colors (or any other flower which comes in more than one color).*

"I've brought some flowers today. Does anyone know what kind they are?" Right away several of the children tell me they are lilacs. "Are they all lilacs?" I question. The children assure me they are, even though they are of three different colors.

"When I was small," I continue, "in fact, until just a few years ago, I thought all lilacs were this light purple color. It's a color which is sometimes called lilac or lavender. Then, not too many years ago, someone gave me some white lilacs. I admired the flowers and asked what they were.

" 'They're lilacs,' the person told me.

" 'No,' I said, 'they can't be lilacs; lilacs are lavender.'

" 'No, some lilacs are white,' the person assured me. 'These are white lilacs.'

"I was really surprised. For nearly forty years I had thought lilacs only came in one color.

"Yesterday, another person gave me a whole bunch of lilacs, half of them white, and half of them this dark purple." I point to the flowers I've brought as I speak. "Once again, I was surprised; once again I learned that lilacs don't have to be lilac-colored. They can also be white — or purple.

"As I was looking at these flowers this morning, I realized that sometimes we think of people in the same way I thought about lilacs for so many years: we expect them to be just one particular way, and if they are not what we expect, we think they're not right

67

or no good. But we know all of these flowers are good, beautiful lilacs, even though they're not all exactly alike.

"Jesus taught us this same thing about people. In Jesus' time and in ours, there are people which culture has judged as not good enough. Maybe they are dirty, or poor, or have done something wrong and we would rather not do things with them. But such differences didn't matter to Jesus. He went looking for the folks who society judged as not good enough, the poor, the blind, the lame, the mentally ill, persons who had done things that were wrong. He even invited people like that to sit down and eat with him! Differences of clean and dirty, rich and poor, good and bad, didn't bother Jesus. He didn't judge people by how they looked or by any of the many ways in which we might judge someone. So, even when society cast such people out, Jesus accepted them, sat down with them, talked with them, ate with them, and said to them, with his words and his deeds, 'God loves you too, just the way you are.'

"That's something I hope you will always remember. No matter what you may have done, no matter what you look like, no matter how different you are from what most people call normal, God loves you anyway, just the way you are."

Prayer: "God, thank you for the many flowers that are blooming throughout the city and countryside, flowers that remind us of our differences. No two of us are exactly alike. We each see the world in our own special way. Help us to be comfortable with the wonder of our differences. Help us to understand that, like the flowers, you created us and love us just the way we are. Amen."

Inextinguishable Light

"Blessed are those who are persecuted for righteousness' sake, for theirs is the kingdom of heaven." — Matthew 5:10

Theme: *Light; darkness; love; hatred.*

Visual Aid: *A "magic" birthday candle (the type that relights itself when it is blown out) inserted in a muffin or cupcake.*

"This morning I'd like you to help me understand the last of the Beatitudes. Jesus said, 'Blessed are those who are persecuted for righteousness' sake, for theirs is the kingdom of heaven.' 'Persecute' is a big word, isn't it? Does anyone know what it means?"

Most of the children sit in silence but one of the older ones suggests that "persecute" means to pester someone. This elicits other responses: to be mean to someone, to be hateful to other people. I agree with the children and point out that the reason people get persecuted is usually because they have ideas which disagree with majority opinion. "That, in fact, is what happened to the early Christians who were persecuted in terrible ways because of their belief in Jesus — and their expression of that belief.

"Jesus told his followers, 'Blessed are you when people persecute you and say all manner of evil things against you for my sake.'[1] He said this to them because he knew how people were going to treat them."

"Not me!" announces a young lady on the front row. "I don't hate God! I believe in God!"

"I'm sure you do, Amanda," I answer. "But some people do not. And persecution and hatred are some of the dark things in life that all of us will run into at some time. However, we also have light in our lives. I'd like you to look around the sanctuary and see all the candles that are here this morning. Over there we have the

Advent candles. In the windows we have candles with the Christmas decorations. On the altar we have two big white candles. And ..."

As I pause, I reveal the candle I have been concealing in my hand. It is a birthday candle, inserted in a cupcake. The children's eyes widen with increased interest. I ask one child to hold the cupcake while I light the candle it holds.

"We seem to have a lot of candles in the sanctuary this morning," I note. "Why are candles so important?" I should have seen the first response coming ...

"Because they're for birthdays!"

"That's one reason," I agree. "What else?"

"Because they're for Christmas!

"Because they light the dark."

"Because they represent Jesus."

Now we are getting somewhere. "Birthdays, Christmas, dark, and Jesus ... Whose birthday is Christmas?" I ask.

"Jesus'!" the children tell me.

"And who lights up the dark places in life?" I continue.

"Jesus!" they answer again.

"That's right," I agree. "Jesus said, 'I am the light of the world.'[2] In the Gospel of John, it is written that 'the light shines in the darkness, and the darkness did not overcome it.'[3] What happens when you put a light in the dark?" I ask.

"You see the light," several children answer.

"So, which is stronger, the light or the dark?"

"The light!" comes their unanimous response.

"Well," I continue, "that suggests to me that if hatred and mean-ness are darknesses, they can be overcome by the light of Jesus." To illustrate this idea of light being stronger than darkness, I ask one of the children to blow out the birthday candle. She does — but it's a trick candle, and in a few seconds it is once again burning brightly.

"Trick candle!" several of the older children announce.

"Yes," I agree, "it's a trick candle.[4] It's a candle made a spe-cial way — with a light so strong you can't blow it out. And that's how God's love is. No matter how mean someone is to you or how mean you may be to someone else, God's love is going to keep on shining. That's why God sent us Jesus, the light of the world — to tell us how much we are loved. And nothing we human beings do to one another can ever separate us from that love. It's not good to hate one another. It's not good to be mean to one another. It's not good to *persecute* one another. But as long as you live as rightly as you are able, with the love of God in your heart, you will be blessed. That's what Jesus meant when he said, 'Blessed are those who are persecuted for righteousness' sake, for theirs is the kingdom of heaven.' "

---

1. Matthew 5:11.

2. John 8:12.

3. John 1:5.

4. It is wise to have a glass of water available to extinguish the candle when this children's sermon is concluded.

"Forgive Us Our Debts"

"And forgive us our debts, as we also have forgiven our debtors."   — Matthew 6:12

Theme: *Forgiveness.*

Visual Aid: *Several large rubber bands.*

————————————

As I greet the children this morning, I pull several rubber bands out of my pocket. The children's eyes light up with interest as they consider the possibilities of what I might be going to do with something so potentially fun.

"I see some of you have noticed the rubber bands I've brought with me. I need someone to take hold of one of them and pull on it just a little bit while I hold onto it too." One of the children volunteers.

As we stretch the rubber band out before the other children, I continue talking. "Stretching a rubber band like this causes what we call 'tension,' " I tell them. "What would happen if Jason and I were to cause too much tension, if we were to stretch it too far?"

"The rubber band would break!" several children respond at once.

"Yes, it would break. And it would probably snap one or both of us on the fingers too! That might sting!"

With these words I notice Jason easing up on the vigor of his pull. I look him in the eye, see his grin, and grin back. We understand that we have the potential to hurt one another here.

"Well, boys and girls, in the Lord's Prayer, there is a sentence which says, 'Forgive us our debts, as we forgive our debtors.' Have any of you ever done anything for which you needed to be forgiven?"

Some of the children take a sudden interest in their shoes with this question; some nod affirmatively, looking uncomfortable; one "smart aleck" says, "Nope!"

"No?!" I question with surprise. "Not ever in your whole life? Are you SURE?"

"Well, maybe ..."

"It's not a good feeling is it?" I ask them all. "It's not a good feeling to need to be forgiven for something. And it's even more difficult to go to the person from whom you need the forgiveness and to ask him for it, isn't it?"

"Yeah, that's REALLY hard," one child agrees.

"Well, what about anger?" I continue. "Have any of you ever been angry with someone?" This time there are no smart replies as the children acknowledge their past angers. "You know, sometimes it's just as difficult to let go of our anger with another person as it is to have to go ask someone to forgive us. The feelings we have in those situations we sometimes call tension — when our feelings are stretched tight just like Jason and I stretched the rubber band a few minutes ago. And remember, we decided if we stretched the rubber band too much it would break!" Young eyes widen as the children begin to make connections between tension on a rubber band and tension caused by anger or a need to be forgiven.

"That's why it's so important to let go of our anger and forgive those who offend us, or to ask for forgiveness if we are the ones who have angered or hurt another. If we don't, the tension mounts. If the tension gets too great, something inside of us breaks, just like the rubber band would have if we had pulled on it harder. That hurts not only us but also the other person or persons involved in the situation. That's why Jesus taught us to pray, 'Forgive us our debts, as we forgive our debtors.' All of us know how painful it is to need to be forgiven and how difficult it is to ask for forgiveness. Perhaps the next time you are angered or hurt by someone you can put yourself in his shoes for a moment and find it in your hearts to forgive him without making him ask. If you can, you'll find that it is a gift to you too."

Help!

"During the night Paul had a dream in which he saw a man standing on the shore of Macedonia pleading, 'Come, help us!'"
— Acts 16:9

Theme: *Helping others; trust.*

Visual Aid: *None. This children's sermon uses the involvement of the entire congregation to capture the children's attention. (NOTE: The ingenuity of this message is that its point can be made whether or not anyone from the congregation responds.)*

"Good morning!" I greet the children. "I need some help this morning." Their eyes widen with interest and a trace of alarm. What might I ask them to do? "Will you help me out?" The only response is a "Maybe!" from one of the boys.

"Well, let's see what happens if I ask someone else ..." I then get up from where I have been kneeling in front of the children and turn to the congregation. "I really DO need help with the children's sermon this morning. Will any of you come up here and help me?"

A motionless, stunned silence greets my plea. No doubt questions are racing through their minds like, "What will she ask me to do if I go up there?" "Will I be embarrassed?"

"No, I'm not kidding, folks. I really DO need help. Is there not even one person among you who will come up here?" Then a number of people start forward, including one entire family of four, the youngest of which has just recently "outgrown" the children's sermon.

"All right!" I hear myself exclaim when I see this response.

"Where do you want us?" asks the first person to arrive.

"Right here on the steps with the children," I reply. When my "volunteers" are seated, I reassure them. "Thank you for coming.

That is all I needed you to do — and you did it, without knowing what I wanted.

"Your presence makes a number of points. For one thing, it emphasizes that God's message is for people of all ages, adults and children, and sometimes it's important to listen and discover together. Additionally, your coming shows your willingness to help, no matter what. You had no idea what I might have asked you to do. And that's the third thing your presence tells us — that you trust me. You trusted me not to embarrass you thoroughly nor ask something of you that was ridiculous or impossible.

"When Paul was on his second missionary journey, he had a dream in which he saw a man on the shore of a country called Macedonia. The man was pleading with Paul, saying, 'Come, help us.' And Paul, trusting that his dream was important, went to Macedonia. This could not have been easy. He had to go by boat, and he wasn't sure who or what he would find when he arrived. He wasn't sure just what sort of help the people of Macedonia might need from him. But he was sure of the love of Christ which he carried in his heart. And it was out of that love that he made the trip to Macedonia.

"When he arrived, he met a woman named Lydia at a place called Philippi. When Lydia heard Paul's message about Jesus, she and her entire household became Christians and the Philippian church was born. Looking around this group, I see that one entire family — an entire household — has joined us this morning. When one member came, the others came too. That's what happened at Philippi — all because Paul listened to a cry for help. When we are asked for help, it may be important to take the attitude these folks took today: 'I'll help you if I can.' For you never know what result God might bring out of your willingness to be there for someone in need. Sometimes just your willingness itself is enough to make a difference."

Helping Hands

"But Jesus said to the disciples, 'Don't send them away. You give them something to eat.' "   — Matthew 14:16

Theme: Discipleship; God's providence; sharing.

Visual Aid: None. The "aid" in this instance is action.

It's one of those Sundays on which I have decided to risk doing something different with the children in order to illustrate the point of the message. So, after the youngsters have gathered on the chancel steps, I turn my back to them and begin speaking. "Well, I guess everyone's here. Good morning."

Not surprisingly, none of them respond. Still facing away from the children, I continue, "Did none of you hear me? I said, 'Good morning.' "

This time one boy answers brightly, "Good morning!"

With his response, I turn around. Now facing the youngsters, I ask them, "How did you feel when I turned my back on you?"

"I don't know," one child replies.

"It didn't matter," says another, eliciting laughter from the congregation.

"At first you didn't answer me," I point out. "Was that because I wasn't looking at you and you weren't sure if I was even talking to you?" Their little heads nod agreement.

"One time when Jesus was out in the countryside, a large crowd gathered to hear him speak. In fact, there were more than 5,000 people there. Do you suppose he turned his back when he talked to them?" The thought of this makes the children grin as they shake their heads to indicate no.

"Well, by the time Jesus got through talking to the crowd, the disciples and all the people were getting hungry. The disciples asked Jesus to send the people away to go find food for themselves. But Jesus told the disciples, 'No, don't send them away. You give them something to eat.' In other words, Jesus said, 'Don't turn your back on them; it's up to you to help them out.'

" 'How can we?' the disciples asked him. 'There are thousands of people here and we only have five loaves of bread and two fish.'

"Do you know what Jesus did then?" I ask the children. My question is greeted by silent, expectant stares, so I continue.

"Jesus said for the disciples to bring him the loaves and the fish. And then he gave some to each of the disciples and said for them to distribute it among the crowd. And you know, there was enough for everyone there. In fact, after everyone had eaten, the disciples gathered up the leftovers — twelve baskets full!

"This story tells us that God needs our help sometimes in order to get things done. Sometimes, our hands are all that God has to use — just as Jesus needed the disciples to feed the people. Do you know anyone right now who might need something to eat?"

Since we were talking about all this the Sunday after the record Midwestern flood in the summer of 1993, the children immediately suggested the flood victims.

"What else might they need besides food?" I ask.

"Shelter ... cleaning supplies ..." The children pause then, thinking.

"What are you wearing?" I ask to prod their thoughts.

"Oh! Clothes! They probably need clothes too!" the children answer.

"That's right," I agree. "And it may seem with so many people needing so many things that helping out is a big job. But another thing this story tells us is that God has a way of taking whatever we have and making it enough, even though it may not seem like enough to us. All that God asks is that we share whatever we have.

"So, there are three things we've learned from this story:

1. God doesn't ever turn his back on us.

2. God takes whatever we have and makes it enough, just as Jesus did with the two fish and the five loaves.

3. God needs us to give help and love to one another. A long time ago, a very wise lady named Teresa of Avila said, 'God has no hands but our hands.' What she meant was that God needs us to accomplish God's work. We often talk about how we need God. It's important to remember that God needs us too."

In Praise Of God

"O come, let us sing unto the Lord: let us make a joyful noise to the rock of our salvation."   — Psalm 95:1

Theme: *Joyful noises; praise.*

Visual Aid: *Handbells and percussion instruments.*

———————————

On this particular Sunday the children's choir, the youth bell choir, and the adult chancel choir are all scheduled to participate in morning worship. It seems a reasonable day on which to talk about praising God with joyful noise.

Knowing I may cause some parents' hearts to beat a bit faster with my first question, I ask the assembled children, "Have any of you ever received advice from your parents about how to act in church?" Immediately heads begin to nod in the affirmative; a few grins appear.

"It looks like most of you have," I continue. "What did your parents tell you?"

"To sit STILL!" one young man offers. Several others agree. "What else?" I ask.

"To shut up!" replies a boy on the front row. This was a little more harsh than I was anticipating, but probably a direct quote. I start to soften his words as I repeat them over the microphone for those who couldn't hear his answer, but catch myself just in time. I have learned that if I'm going to reiterate what the children have said, it is best to keep it in their words. The alternative is to have them say, "That's not what I said."

"To sit STILL and shut up!" My announcement is greeted with general laughter throughout the sanctuary. "Well, I'm sure all of you follow that advice, don't you?" The smaller children look very earnest as they indicate agreement; the older ones squirm a bit and grin, knowing no one ever sits completely still, completely quiet during worship.

"You know, even adults don't always manage to follow that advice," I suggest. This brings more knowing grins to some of their faces as they contemplate the apparent double standard of who is allowed to talk in church and who is not.

Redirecting their attention I ask, "What do you see on top of these tables here in the front of the sanctuary?"

"Bells!" comes the immediate reply.

"Yes, handbells," I affirm.

"Do bells make noise?" I question.

"Of course!"

"Yes!"

"They ring!"

It would seem that bells definitely make noise.

"And on this table over here we have some other percussion instruments the children's choir will be using at the end of our service. These make noise too. In fact, some of *you* will be using them to make noise — right here in church!

"What kind of noises are these? Are they rude noises?" Little heads shake negatively.

"Are they noises that interrupt something else that is going on?"

"Only if someone rings them at the wrong time," a wise little girl points out.

"So, what kind of noises are they?"

"Good noises!"

"Fun noises!"

"Could you say they were joyful noises?" I ask. The children nod agreement. "What are other joyful noises we make?"

"Singing," comes an obvious response.

"Praying," is offered as another. I realize the children are focusing on what *usually* goes on in church. Suddenly I start clapping my hands together, bringing more grins from the children. "Do you ever do that?" I ask.

"Yes!"

"When I like something."

"That's right," I agree. "When someone sings well, or plays well, or speaks well, sometimes we clap to show our appreciation — even in church.

"Do any of you ever whistle?" I ask. Some of the children indicate they do, but none of them purse their lips to perform. I realize they continue to suffer the effects of the almost ingrained instructions to "sit STILL and shut up!" So, I whistle a few bars of "Jesus Loves Me" and indicate they can try whistling too, right now, right here in church, if they want to. And, much to my delight, some do.

"What other sorts of noises do you sometimes make, noises that are filled with joy? What do you do when something seems funny?"

"Oh!" they say as if surprised they had not thought of it sooner, "we laugh!"

"Yes!" I agree. "Laughter is a noise that bubbles with joy.

"Why are joyful noises important? Why do we make them in church? Why do we sing, and applaud, and laugh, and play instruments, maybe even whistle?"

"To praise God!"

"To tell God we love him."

"Because it feels good."

"Because it's fun."

"Because our choir director tells us to."

These are but some of the responses.

"Yes, for all of those reasons. And I want to emphasize what I heard from some of you: that we make joyful noises to praise God. We come here to worship God, to honor God, together, as a community. This week, whenever you find yourself singing, or whistling, or clapping, or so excited about something that you jump up and down or dance around — whenever you find yourself making a joyful noise, I hope you'll remember what we talked about today and know that God hears your noise and appreciates your praise."

Light

"Jesus said to them, 'The light is with you for a little longer. Walk while you have the light, so that the darkness may not overtake you. If you walk in the darkness, you do not know where you are going.' " — John 12:35

Theme: Decisions; light; discernment.

Visual Aid: A camera with fairly fast film.

To explore this text with the children I have brought a camera with fairly high-speed film in it. Once the children have gathered for this portion of worship, I ask as I hold the camera aloft, "What did I bring to share with you today?"

"A CAMERA!" comes their immediate response.

"And what does one do with a camera?" I question.

"You take pictures!" the children reply with assurance.

"Oh!" I say as if surprised or puzzled. "Well, if that's the case, shall I take your picture?" Interestingly enough, I discover at this point that not all children are hams when it comes to cameras. Some of them definitely do not want their picture taken.

"Do it democratically!" one boy suggests.

"Okay," I tell them, "let's take a vote. Everyone who wants your picture taken, please raise your hand." About half the children do so. (No one ever said doing children's sermons was necessarily easy or without surprises. What to do now was the next question I had for myself.)

"All right. Everyone who wants to have me take your picture move over to this side of the steps." I motion them to move to their right. "The rest of you come over to this other side."

The children move to their new places. As I point the camera towards those who want their picture taken, I suggest that they smile. Then I snap the shutter. With mock surprise I look at the camera and back at the children. "Did the flash go off?" I ask them (knowing it hadn't because the film speed was fast enough to cope with indoor light).

"There was no flash," the children tell me.

"Well, do you think I should take it again to be sure it comes out?"

"Yes!" come their immediate replies.

This time I turn on the "fillflash" mechanism so the flash works when I take the next picture. That accomplished, I ask, "Why was the flash important?"

"So there'd be enough light," several children answer.

"That's right," I continue. "But it's not dark in here this morning, is it?"

"No, we have the lights," someone points out.

"And there's light from the sun coming in the windows," another child replies.

Immediately I switch the subject with the question, "Have any of you ever been camping?" Many of the children nod.

"Everyone who has been camping, please raise your hand." All but two of them do so.

"Have any of you ever gotten up in the middle of the night when you were camping?" Again there are several nods.

"Well, wasn't it dark?" I ask. "How did you see?"

"I had a flashlight!"

"Used a flashlight!"

"Turned on the flashlight!" The operative word here is definitely "flashlight."

"Well, there it is again," I continue, "the need for light. It's pretty hard for us to see in the dark or to take pictures in the dark isn't it?" The children agree.

"You know, Jesus had many names for himself. He called himself 'the bread of the world,' he called himself 'living water.' What else did he call himself?" With this lead-in it isn't difficult for some of the older children to come up with the answer I'm seeking.

"The light of the world!" they tell me.

"Yes, 'the light of the world.' We've talked about how diffi-cult it is to do things in the dark because we cannot see. Some-times we experience the same sort of thing mentally when we have to make a tough decision. We feel like we are walking through darkness and can't find the right path or don't know which way to turn. It's at those times that it is important to remember we don't have to try to find our way without help. We have Jesus, the light of the world, to show us the choice he would have us make, to show us the path he would have us follow. The next time you have a difficult decision facing you, perhaps you'll remember what we talked about today; perhaps you'll take the problem to Jesus and let him help you decide what to do."

Amazing Grace

"Always be ready to answer, with gentleness and understanding, anyone who asks of you a reason for the hope that is within you."   — 1 Peter 3:15b

Theme: *Grace.*

Visual Aid: *A blank piece of paper and a box of crayons.*

As the children note the blank sheet of white paper I have placed on the floor in front of them I ask, "Does anyone here like to draw?" Grins break out on their faces, heads nod affirmatively, and some hands go up.

"I see some of you raising your hands. What about the rest of you? If you like to draw, raise your hand." Immediately every child on the chancel steps has a hand raised, some of them flailing rather wildly to indicate the intensity of their interest.

Watching their faces now eager with anticipation, I reach into my pocket to retrieve a box of crayons. The children's eyes widen momentarily as they recognize my treasure. "What have I brought today?" I ask them.

"Crayons!" comes their united reply.

"And what else?" I ask, looking toward the floor.

"Paper!" they answer.

"Well, now, that suggests maybe I ought to draw something on the paper, doesn't it?" The children agree.

Quickly I select a dark color and render a crude outline of an animal: two ovals, a tail, ears, whiskers, stick legs. I hold it up for their review. "Does anyone know what this is?"

"A cat!" they respond. It is reassuring that most of them seem to recognize my efforts.

"Yes, it's a cat," I agree. "Now, what if I were to go over there (I point to indicate where) and draw a cat on the side of that pew?" The children could not look more horrified. Their eyes stare at me in wild disbelief as their mouths fall open in speechless amazement that I would even suggest such a thing.

"Ahhhhhh!" I draw in an audible, deep breath as I mimic their expressions of surprise. "Would that be an all right thing to do?" I ask.

"NO!" comes their vehement response.

"Do you think I might get in trouble?"

"YES!" they answer with certainty.

"Well, you can relax," I continue. "I'm not going to draw on the pew. But I would like to tell you a story about something I did when I was three years old. My parents had just had the inside walls of our house painted. My mother was in the kitchen doing one of the many things moms do in kitchens. I was in the living room, coloring. I must have been aware that my parents had gone to some amount of trouble to get the walls painted. Or maybe it was just the large expanse of fresh, white surface that I found irresistible. But, guess what I did?"

"You didn't draw on the WALL, did you?" one child asks, almost too shocked to voice the question.

"Yes," I answer, "that's exactly what I did. And *then*, I went into the kitchen, took my mother's hand, and started pulling her toward the living room to show her what I had done. You see, I was too young to understand that it wasn't a good thing to do. I thought I had done something wonderful; it was a present for my mother.

"She must have been very surprised and very unhappy when I showed her the newly 'decorated' wall. But the most amazing thing is, she didn't get angry! She knew I was too young to understand that I had done something wrong. Actually, I was too young even to remember this happening. However, she told me this story often as I was growing up, when I *was* old enough to know the difference between right and wrong and to answer for what I did or didn't do. She told me the story to remind me that even when I did something wrong she still loved me. And you know, God is like that too, loving us even when we do things we shouldn't. Like my mother that day I drew on the wall, God may not like everything we do, but no matter what, God loves us. That's what grace is all about — and it truly is amazing."

A Basket Of Angels

"And suddenly there was a great earthquake; for an angel of the Lord, descending from heaven, came and rolled back the stone from the door and sat on it. His appearance was like lightning and his clothing white as snow." — Matthew 28:2-3

Theme: *God's constant presence; Easter; resurrection.*

Visual aid: *A big basket filled with artificial grass and all the angels I could find among my Christmas decorations.*

It is Easter. I have brought a basket filled with angels as an aid to our discussion of the events at Christ's tomb on Easter morning. The largest angel is almost a foot tall, made of paper. The others are smaller, one of blown glass, one tatted, one made of pieces of macaroni, one of lace. They are Christmas ornaments, but as a friend pointed out when I was putting the basket together, "I would hope that angels are appropriate in church any time." Me too — and not just in church.

When the children have gathered, I ask, "Did anyone have a basket at home this morning?" Several heads nod, a few hands tentatively go up. "Let me see those hands," I encourage. It looks like every one of them got an Easter basket.

"What was in your basket?" I ask one of the children near the microphone. "Nothing!" she announces with satisfaction, much to my surprise and the congregation's amusement.

"Nothing?" I question.

"That's right," she affirms. "It was empty — but I get to hunt for eggs later. Then it will have eggs in it."

I was relieved. As people have often pointed out to me, it's always a risk to ask questions during a children's sermon. But it's a risk worth taking in order to get them involved.

Other children's hands are waving demandingly now as they are eager to tell me what was in their baskets. "I had a *troll* in mine," one child proclaims with glee. Laughter again resonates through the congregation. As I elicit additional responses from other children, the majority of the answers consist of a single sweet word: "CANDY!"

One child is more explicit. "Chocolate eggs!" he announces. And the last response is, *"Beauty and the Beast."* Whether this is a video or a book we don't take time to explore.

My basket has been out of sight during this discussion, waiting under the front pew. Now I reach for it and put it down in the middle of the circle of children.

"I don't seem to have candy, or trolls, or *Beauty and the Beast* in my basket. What do I have?" The children have been eyeing the basket with expressions ranging from curiosity to surprise to wonder.

"Angels!" they respond in chorus.

"Why do you suppose I would have angels in an Easter basket?" I continue.

"Because of the angel at Jesus' tomb on Easter," one of the older children answers.

"How did you know that?" I ask, fairly certain I knew.

"I sang with the children's choir at first service," she responds. Laughter again ripples through the congregation.

"Well, good," I reply, "then you can help me out with the rest of this. You say there was an angel at the tomb. Was Jesus there?"

"No," she answers, "that's why the angel was there, to tell the ladies who came that Jesus had risen."

"That's right," I agree. "The angel was God's messenger, and the message the angel brought wasn't just for the women who came to the tomb; it was a message for all of us, that Jesus is risen; he is alive and with us always.

"You know, angels aren't just for Christmas or Easter. Angels are messengers we may meet any time. They come in all shapes and sizes and remind us that God is with us, Jesus is with us, every moment of every day."

Crumbs

"He answered and said, 'It is not fair to take the children's food and throw it to the dogs.' And she said, 'Yes, Lord. Yet even the dogs eat the crumbs that fall from their masters' table.' "

— Matthew 15:26-27

Theme: *Helping others; sharing.*

Visual Aid: *A saltine cracker in a plastic bag.*

———————————

This is a difficult text even for adults. In order to help the children make some sense out of it, I have brought a saltine cracker in a baggie. I begin by asking the kids, "Do you know what a crumb is?" No one is sure enough to describe a crumb to me, so I take the baggie with the cracker out of my pocket, hold it up and ask, "Is this a crumb?"

"No!" I am told, "It's a cracker!"

"That's right. It's a cracker. But what if I do this...?" With those words I crush the cracker (still in the baggie to contain the crumbs). "Now," I continue, holding up the crunched pieces, "do I still have a cracker?"

"No, you have a bag of crumbs."

"Aha!" I respond. "So, now we know what a crumb is. It's a piece of something — a very small piece. Crumbs are what is left on your plate when you finish eating a piece of cake. Crumbs are what fall off the loaf when the bread is broken during communion. Crumbs are the little parts no one really misses or cares about, except ... I wonder, do any of you have a pet?"

Many of the children indicate with nods that they do, so I begin asking what these pets might be. As luck would have it, every single one of the children present has a cat. Being particularly fond of cats myself, this would normally not be a problem. But this morning, in view of the lectionary text, we obviously needed to talk about dogs.

"Do any of you have a friend who has a dog?" Several children indicate they do.

"Are these dogs allowed to come in the house?" Again, the response is affirmative.

"Well, if one of these dogs was in the house while the family was eating dinner and if a crumb of food dropped off the table to the floor, what do you suppose would happen to the crumb?"

"The dog would eat it!" comes the instant reply.

"Yes," I agree, "that's what I think would happen too. Now, we've already seen that a crumb is a very small piece of something, so small that usually no one wants it. But we weren't thinking about dogs. Sometimes dogs are very happy to have the crumbs from our tables — the scraps no one else wants.

"We're talking about this today because of a conversation Jesus had with a woman who asked him for some help. Jesus told her, 'It's not right for me to take the children's food and throw it to the dogs.' Then the woman replied, 'Even the dogs get to eat the crumbs that fall from their master's table.'

"What she meant by saying that to him was that she didn't need very much. All she was asking for was what no one else would want or miss — just a crumb. So Jesus gave her what she needed.

"You know, sometimes we have things in our lives we don't want — not crumbs exactly, but toys we don't play with anymore, clothes we've grown out of and don't wear anymore, things we might throw away that someone else might use. Things that seem like trash to us may be a real treasure to someone else. This story about Jesus and the woman tells us we need to be aware of how little it takes sometimes to fill another's need; sometimes just a few crumbs are enough."

Listening

"That same day Jesus went out of the house and sat beside the sea. Such great crowds gathered around him that he got into a boat and sat there, while the whole crowd stood on the beach. And he told them many things in parables, saying: 'Listen! A sower went out to sow. And as he sowed, some seeds fell on the path, and the birds came and ate them up. Other seeds fell on rocky ground, where they did not have much soil, and they sprang up quickly, since they had no depth of soil. But when the sun rose, they were scorched; and since they had no root, they withered away. Other seeds fell among thorns, and the thorns grew up and choked them. Other seeds fell on good soil and brought forth grain, some a hundredfold, some sixty, some thirty. Let anyone with ears listen!' "
— Matthew 13:1-9

Theme: *Awareness; paying attention.*

Visual Aid: *A plastic bag containing sunflower seeds.*

"Why are you here this morning?" I ask the children who have assembled on the chancel steps — at my invitation. My question is met with silence and wide-eyed uncertainty as laughter erupts from the congregation. "My goodness!" I exclaim. "Has my question left you speechless? Why did you come up to the steps just now?" I inquire, fully expecting at least one child might say, "Because you asked us to." But whether it's a case of it's-early-on-a-summer-morning-and-I'm-not-awake-yet or simply an unusual shyness for this bunch, the children remain silent.

"Could it be that you came up here to listen to something?" I continue. Finally a few heads nod in agreement. Then I hold up a bag I've brought with me and ask the children what it contains.

"Sunflower seeds!" several reply.

"Well, suppose I wanted to plant these seeds to grow sunflowers," I suggest. "What would happen if I just went out and scattered them on the ground?"

"The birds would eat them!" comes the response.

"That's right," I agree. "Birds like sunflower seeds. What if I threw them into some rocks?"

"They wouldn't grow," the children assure me.

"No, they can't grow in rocks. Seeds need dirt in which to grow. What if I threw them into a field that was already full of weeds and thorns?"

"They might grow, but they'd have trouble because of the other stuff," says one child.

"So, what do I have to do to be sure they take root and grow into sunflowers?" I ask.

"Plant them in soil that doesn't have other stuff growing in it and that isn't full of rocks." These children catch on quickly.

"So, what you're telling me is that I need to be careful where I plant them; that I need to put them in good soil. Did you know that Jesus told a story like this, about a person who went out to plant seeds? Some of it spilled on the ground and, sure enough, the birds ate it, just as you suggested they would. And some of the seeds fell among rocks where they sprouted but couldn't sink their roots in to really grow. So, when the sun came out, the plants in the rocks withered and died. Some of the seeds fell among thorns and the thorns choked out the plants that sprouted. But some of the seeds fell on good soil, soil that had been prepared to receive them. What do you think happened to those seeds?"

"They grew!" There was no doubt in this response.

"That's right, they grew. And the person who planted them got a good crop. But there's something else about this story that is interesting. Did you know that when Jesus told it he really wasn't talking about planting seeds at all?" This brings surprised, puzzled looks to the children's faces. "What Jesus was talking about was listening; he was talking about what you all came up here to do." The children look more puzzled than ever; after all, metaphor is a difficult concept sometimes, at any age.

"Let me explain. In Jesus' story, the seeds are words, God's words. The soil is people like you and me. It's important for us to be good soil so God's words can take root in us and grow. So the question then is, how can we be good soil? How can we receive the words of God?"

"By listening?" one child asks.

"Yes, by listening," I agree. "And just as the soil has to be prepared to receive the seed, we have to be prepared to listen, to receive the words of God, whether they come to us through the Bible or through another person.

"You know, God speaks to us in many ways, and not always with actual words. Sometimes God speaks to us through the beauty of a sunset or through the kindness of another person. But we won't hear God unless we are aware, unless we are ready to listen.

"How many of you have ever had someone say to you, 'You aren't listening to me!'" Several hands go up in response. "Who has said that to you in the past?" I ask, suspecting I know the answer.

"My parents," comes the unanimous reply.

"And have you ever said that to them?" Some of the children look shocked at this suggestion, but others nod agreement. "How

do you feel when someone doesn't listen to what you're trying to say to them?" The children agree they don't like it.

"It's important to pay attention when someone wants us to listen, just as we want people to pay attention to us when we want them to listen. And it's the same way with God. God always listens to us; sometimes we don't listen to God. If we don't listen, we are like the hard ground, or the rocks, or the soil growing thorns; if we don't listen, God's words cannot take root in us and grow into the love and compassion which are its fruits."

I thank the children for coming and we have a short prayer before they go back to their seats: "God, thank you for giving us the ears to hear your words, the eyes to see your words, the hands to feel your words. Thank you for making us good soil in which your words and your love can sprout and grow as we share them with one another. Amen."

Strength In Meekness

"Blessed are the meek, for they will inherit the earth."
— Matthew 5:5

Theme: *Flexibility; strength; healing; mending.*

Visual Aid: *A very large blade of grass (about an inch wide and fifteen inches long) and a branch or stick.*

———————

"We have been talking about the Beatitudes the last few weeks. This morning, I'd like to discuss another one with you. Jesus said, 'Blessed are the meek, for they shall inherit the earth.' Does anybody know what 'meek' means?" The children look thoughtful, but none offers an answer. "Is it a word you have heard?" I ask, hoping they are at least familiar with its sound, if not its meaning. The children nod affirmatively, so I continue.

" 'Meek' can mean 'gentle.' It can mean 'not very strong.' It can mean 'timid' or 'shy.' Sometimes 'meek' is used to describe a person who is easily pushed around. Meekness is generally not a quality that we in our culture tend to admire."

"I've brought a couple of things with me this morning to help us try to understand the word 'meek.' I've brought a stick and a large blade of grass. Now, of these two, which would you call 'meek?' "

With little hesitation, several children respond: "The grass!"

"Do the rest of you agree?" I ask. They do.

Affirming their responses, I pose a rhetorical question: "The grass doesn't look like it's as strong as the stick, does it?" Then I ask one of the children to take hold of one end of the stick and pull while I hang on to the other end.

"This stick seems strong," I note. "At least, it didn't break."

Next I ask another child to pull on one end of the grass. It is a hefty piece of grass — and hadn't pulled apart when I tested it earlier. But grace has a way of taking over in the midst of a children's sermon, enlarging upon or deepening the message I've brought to the youngsters. This morning is no exception. As the child pulls the grass away from me, it breaks! One part of my mind considers what to do about this unexpected circumstance while another part continues our conversation.

"When we pulled on the grass, it broke into two pieces. But what if you wanted to bend the grass? Would that cause it to break?" The children tell me it would not.

"What if I try to bend the stick?"

"It will break," the children assure me. So, I bend the stick until it snaps.

"Sure enough, the stick broke," I continue. "From our experience so far we can see that the grass and the stick have different kinds of strength. The stick can be pulled on without breaking; the grass can be bent without breaking — and it's a little easier to fix the grass. We can tie it back together because it has the kind of strength that allows it to bend.[1] But how are we going to fix the stick?"

"Glue it together?" Beverly questions.

"What if I don't have any glue?" I respond.

"Tape it," Marty suggests.

"Like the glue, tape would work if I had some; but I don't. Is there a way I could fix the stick right now, with just what I have?"

"With the grass?" comes a meek suggestion from one of the shyest youngsters.

"With the grass! Yes! But I need your help. If you will hold the two pieces of the stick together, I can tie the grass around the broken place ..." In a moment, the stick is again in one piece, more or less.

"I think there is a message for us here, a message about meekness and about binding things together. Which would you say was more like Jesus, the stick or the grass?"[2]

"The grass," several children answer.

"Do you all agree?" The others nod.

"Why do you think the grass is more like Jesus?" I continue. And, as so often, I am blessed by the profound insight of one of our younger theologians:

"We can break Jesus by hurting his heart — and we know the grass can be broken in two. Jesus also mends our broken places, like you fixed the broken stick with the grass. And you fixed the grass by tying it back together. We can be nice to Jesus and that mends his heart. When we're nice to each other, it mends his heart too."

I thank the children for sharing their thoughts and bring our time together to a close: "Sometimes Jesus was called 'meek.' But, as you can see, there's a different kind of strength in being meek, a quiet strength that people seldom see. It's a strength that can bend when it needs to and bind together the broken places in our lives."

---

1. I demonstrate this "mending" by tying the two pieces of grass together as I continue to speak.

2. It's always risky to ask such a question, for the children just might see things differently than I do. But that's why I continue to ask them. For when the children respond with an unexpected answer, I always have my perspective broadened.

Peanuts For Breakfast

"For one believes that he may eat all things; another, who is weak, eats only vegetables. Let the one who eats not despise the one who does not, nor the one who does not eat despise the one who does; for the Lord receives everyone. Who are you to judge another man's servant?... No one lives to himself; no one dies to himself. When we live, we live to the Lord; when we die, we die unto the Lord; whether we live, therefore, or die, we are the Lord's."
— Romans 14:2-4a, 7-8

Theme: *Differences; tolerance.*

Visual Aid: *None, though two possibilities include a cereal bowl and a donut.*

It seemed to me, as I thought about this text, that the best way to get its message across to young children would be to discuss with them what they each ate for breakfast; surely they would not all have eaten the same thing. But I failed to factor in one detail of the morning's activities: during the church school hour there was an all-church breakfast. Of course, by the time I realized this, my route to helping the children discover the meaning of the text was already planned, so I followed it despite the unexpected turn events had taken. It is the nature of grace that following my intuition, what my heart said was right, did, in fact, accomplish the desired objective.

As soon as the children have come to the front of the sanctuary, I ask how many of them went to the breakfast that morning. Virtually all of them raise their hands. "I wonder if you all had the same thing to eat," I continue. "How many of you had eggs?" No hands are raised. "How many of you had bread?" Still no hands. "Surely you didn't have cereal?" I question, trying to recall if cereal was even available.

Like a bubble rising to the top of a pool of water, a word suddenly bursts from several of the children simultaneously: "Donuts!" No wonder I have not suggested the right thing — by the time I had gotten to the breakfast, all the donuts were gone. Of course they ate donuts — and, of course, all of them ate the same thing. It was time to bring in other breakfasts.

"Today was a special day at our church, when we all ate breakfast together. But on a usual day, what do you eat for breakfast?" I ask hopefully. "Cereal," comes the reply — from every single child present. "Okay," I think to myself, "We can use this ..."

"I got up really early this morning," I continue. "I was very hungry, so I had a bowl of cereal before I came. When you eat cereal, what do you put on it?"

"Milk," comes the again unanimous response.

"I put milk on mine too. Do you put anything else on yours?" I ask.

The children look thoughtful, even a bit perplexed, as they ponder what else one might put on one's cereal. "Do you mean to tell me I am the only person here who puts peanuts on her cereal in the morning?"[1] Surprised, the children laughingly agree.

Having gotten across that difference between us, I go on to point out others. I note that their shoes are all different, their hair colors and hair cuts are different. I ask them to look around the congregation and note the differences they see in the people gathered for worship.

"We don't all look alike," I suggest as they continue to look around. "We don't all eat alike. We don't all sound alike. We probably don't all think alike. God has created us with differences. And yet we are all God's children. We are all a part of this community we know as church, gathered here to worship God — the God who made us to be who we are and to love one another just as we are, for that's how God loves us."

---

1. I really did at that time!

Tears

"When Mary came where Jesus was and saw him, she knelt at his feet and said to him, 'Lord, if you had been here, my brother would not have died.' When Jesus saw her weeping, and the Jews who came with her also weeping, he was greatly disturbed in spirit and deeply moved. He said, 'Where have you laid him?' They said to him, 'Lord, come and see.' Jesus began to weep. So the Jews said, 'See how he loved him.' " — John 11:32-36

Theme: *Crying; self-esteem; love; friendship.*

Visual Aid: *An onion.*

"This morning I have brought something all of you will probably recognize. What is it?" I hold up a round object for all to see.

"An onion!" the children reply, some of them wrinkling their noses in disgust.

"Ah, yes ... an onion." I pause for a moment looking at it with them. "What do you suppose would happen if I were to peel this onion and cut it up?"

"Gosh! It would STINK!" exclaims one of the boys. The others nod in agreement.

"So you don't think I should do that?"

"NO!" comes their definite response.

"Okay, I won't. But what if I did? What would happen besides creating a strong smell?"

"It might make you cry?" one of the children answers tentatively.

"Yes, it might cause me to cry. You see, some of the same particles that would be released to cause the smell of the onion might also get in my eyes and make them sting. My eyes would water; they'd get tears in them to wash out the onion fumes.

"That's one of the reasons God gave us the ability to cry. Tears help us protect our eyes from things that might hurt them. But that's not the only reason we sometimes cry, is it? What are other reasons we might cry?"

After a brief pause, one child says, "I might cry if I fell down and really got hurt or scared."

"Yes, I can remember doing that many times," I answer. This brings general laughter from the kids and the rest of the congregation as they recall how many times they have seen me on crutches. "What else might make us cry?" I continue.

"Because something makes us sad," comes the next answer, from one of the girls.

"Well, what might make you sad?" I ask.

"Losing something I really care about, I guess," she replies.

So as not to put this one child too much on the spot, I turn my attention to the group at large and ask, "What are some things you might lose that would make you cry if you lost them?"

Favorite toys are among the initial responses, but as I prod a little more the family pets are brought up. "Well, why would you cry if you lost your dog or your cat?"

"Because we LOVE them," the children answer, seeming surprised that I would have to ask.

"Yes, because you love them," I agree. "And you see, that's why Jesus cried when he heard the news that his friend Lazarus was dead — because he loved him.

"You know, sometimes some of us find it hard to cry. Sometimes some of us are embarrassed to cry, especially in front of someone else. I think it's important to remember that tears are one of the ways we express our love and that it's okay to cry; even Jesus did it sometimes."

Turning Around

"Now after John was arrested, Jesus came to Galilee, pro-claiming the good news of God, and saying, 'The time is fulfilled, and the kingdom of God has come near; repent, and believe in the good news.' As Jesus passed along the Sea of Galilee, he saw Simon and his brother Andrew casting a net into the sea — for they were fishermen. And Jesus said to them, 'Follow me and I will make you fish for people.' And immediately they left their nets and followed him. As he went a little farther, he saw James the son of Zebedee and his brother John, who were in their boat mending the nets. Immediately he called to them; and they left their father Zebedee in the boat with the hired men, and followed him."

— Mark 1:14-20

Theme: *Discipleship.*

Visual Aid: *None. The children are involved through experience.*

As the children gather on the chancel steps, they sit down as usual. "Is everyone comfortable?" I ask when they have gotten settled. Several children nod affirmatively. "Well, that's great," I continue, "but I need you to do something different today. I need all of you to stand up please, and turn around."

Dutifully, the children do as they are told (with the exclusion of one free-spirited five-year-old who challenges my directive by standing but not turning around; she confronts me with a broad grin). "Yes, young lady," I respond to her unspoken question, "I want you to turn around too." Having received the individual attention she sought, she joins the other children.

I say nothing more. Seconds tick past in silence. The children begin to fidget. Finally one child looks back over her shoulder, perhaps to see what I'm doing, perhaps to encourage me to get on with things and not just leave her and the others standing there.

I put a finger to my lips to indicate silence, then motion to her with my hands to go ahead and sit down. The other children continue to stand, their fidgets becoming more intense; but they do not turn around. After what seems an eternity (all of 45 seconds have passed) I tell them they can turn around and be seated. Immediately they notice the youngster on the front row who is already sitting.

Responding to their observation, I tell them, "Julia's curiosity overcame her. She turned around while the rest of you stood there. So, without speaking, I motioned to her to sit down. Julia was paying attention to me with her eyes. The rest of you were paying attention with your ears. But because I asked you to do something unusual this morning, you were all paying closer attention than you might have otherwise.

"Our litany this morning opened with these words: 'Come with undivided attention to meet God who calls us from old routines.' That's what happened to the disciples; Jesus called them from their old routines (the things they usually did) to something new.

"Jesus was walking along the seashore where Peter, Andrew, James, and John were all fishing. Jesus said to them, 'Come, follow me, and I will make you fish for people.' Fishing was their routine; fishing was how they earned their living. Now, here was this man whom they had never met saying, 'Come, follow me, and I will turn you into a different sort of fishermen; come, follow me, and I will change your life completely.' And the most amazing thing happened. They *did* follow him!

"Jesus literally turned their lives around. That's why I had you stand up and turn around this morning, to have you experience something completely different than what you are used to; because Jesus calls us to do something different with our lives. He calls us to follow him.

"When I left you standing there this morning, you began to listen more closely for the sound of my voice. The longer I left you in silence, the more you expected me to speak, to tell you what to do next; the longer I left you, the more closely you listened.

"Sometimes it's very important to stop completely, stand very still, and just listen. It's easy to get involved in the routines of our lives, the things we always do the same way, and not really pay attention either to what we are doing or to what God would have us do. Just as Jesus called to the disciples, 'Come, follow me ...' he calls us as well. But unless we pay attention, we may not hear him saying, 'Come, follow me ... Come, follow the example I have set for you to love one another ... and when you do, I will turn your life around; it will never, ever be the same.' "

"... For You"

"...the Lord Jesus on the night when he was betrayed took a loaf of bread, and when he had given thanks, he broke it and said, 'This is my body that is broken for you. Do this in remembrance of me.' In the same way he took the cup also, after supper, saying, 'This cup is the new covenant in my blood. Do this as often as you drink it, in remembrance of me.' "   — 1 Corinthians 11:23b-25

Theme: *Communion; sharing; community; remembering.*

Visual Aid: *A small loaf of bread or a roll and a ceramic glass.*

"Have any of you ever had trouble remembering things?" I ask the assembled children. Heads nod; a few hands go up.

"Raise your hand if you've ever had trouble remembering something." Every child raises a hand; I raise mine too — and have no doubt every adult in the room has mentally done so as well.

"It looks like all of us have this problem sometimes. Do any of you know, or *remember* from discussions you've had in Sunday School or Children's Choir, what is special about this Sunday for the church?"

A five-year-old tentatively raises her hand. When I nod to her, she replies softly, "It's World Communion Sunday."

"That's right. Today is World Communion Sunday. That means that Christians all over the world will celebrate communion today. That sort of bonds all of us together. In fact, that's one of the meanings of communion: bonding together, sharing." As I continue talking with the children, I begin to uncover the bread and small ceramic glass I have brought, wrapped together in a white linen towel.

"You all know that Jesus shared many things with the disciples. And when it came time for him to leave them, he wanted them to

109

remember him. So he thought of a very simple way to get that to happen.

"Jesus and the disciples, his very closest friends, were eating a meal together. It was very common to have bread with their meals; this night was no exception. So, what did Jesus do?" As I ask this question, I reach for the small loaf of bread and hold it up as if I'm going to break it apart.

"He took the bread and broke it," several children answer.

"And did he say anything as he did that?" I ask.

"He said, 'This is my body...?'"

"That's right. He said, 'This is my body.' And he added something else. He said, 'This is my body, broken for ...' who?"

"YOU!" comes a chorus of very definite young voices. In response, I point to each child as I repeat the words again: "Yes, Jesus said, 'This is my body broken for you ... and you ... and you ... and you ...' And he said, 'I want you to eat this bread, and every time you are together to break bread, to eat together, I want you to ...' what?"

After the slightest pause, one child says, "Remember?"

"Yes, 'I want you to remember ... to remember *me*.'"

"Then Jesus took a cup of wine from the table." With these words, I hold up the earthenware glass.

"Just like the bread, wine was something they had with their meals every day. What did Jesus say about the wine?"

"This is my blood ..." several children say softly.

"Yes," I continue. "He said, 'This is my blood, my *life*, poured out for ...' who?"

Once again, the children are very sure of their answer. "For YOU!" comes their response.

"Yes, for *all* of you. And then he told the disciples, 'Every time you sit down to drink together at a meal I want you to ...' what?"

"Remember me!" comes the now unhesitating response.

"Why do you suppose being remembered was so important to him?" I ask. It's one of those questions I hadn't consciously planned to ask, a question that just comes flowing out of me of its own volition. And a nine-year-old child answers:

"Because he thinks we're important and he wants us to think he's just as important as we are." Out of the mouths of babes ... Following her lead, I ask the next thing that comes to mind: "Do you know why Jesus thinks we're important?"

The same young theologian replies, "Because we're all living a life together and we're part of his life." I find myself wanting to sit for the rest of the morning at this child's feet that she might teach me more. But instead, I thank her for her answer and continue.

"Jesus thinks we're important because we do share his life; he thinks we're important because he loves us. By sharing this time together, by singing together, praying together, worshiping together, by being here together, we are with Jesus and he is with us. That's what communion is all about — sharing, being together, being joined in spirit to one another and to Jesus. And it's important for us to re ..." I pause until I hear the united response, "Remember!"

"Yes, it's important for us to remember Jesus in everything we do, to remember him, to remember he loves us, and to remember he needs our love too."

Yahweh

"But Moses said to God, 'If I come to the Israelites and say to them, "The God of your ancestors has sent me to you," and they ask me, "What is his name?" what shall I say to them?' God said to Moses, 'I AM WHO I AM.' He said further, 'Thus you shall say to the Israelites, "I AM has sent me to you." ' "— Exodus 3:13-14

Theme: *Self-esteem.*

Visual Aid: *White posterboard with "YHWH" written in capital letters.*

━━━━━━━━━━━

As the children come up to the front of the sanctuary, I place the posterboard face down in front of me. Following my usual practice, I begin with a question.

"Does everyone here have a name?" This brings laughs and giggles as the children nod. Of *course* everyone has a name! At this point, with a small group, I will ask each child to tell me her/his name.

"Have you ever forgotten someone's name?" Several children indicate they have. "How did that make you feel?" I ask.

"Dumb!" Nancy responds.

"Embarrassed!" offers Matt.

"Once I forgot my OWN name," says George, causing more giggles.

"Has anyone else ever forgotten your name?" I ask him. He nods affirmatively.

"How about the rest of you? Has anyone ever forgotten your name?" Several more children acknowledge this experience.

"How did that make you feel?" I question.

"Like I wasn't very important ..."

"Like they didn't recognize me ..."

"Like they didn't care about me ..."

"And how do you feel when someone remembers your name?" I continue.

"Good!"

"Yes, it feels good to have someone remember our name, doesn't it? Our names give us identity. Our names tell us we are somebody; we exist.

"Did you know that God knows the name of every one of you?" This brings everything from assured nods to looks of surprise.

"And we know lots of names for God, too, don't we? What are some of those names?"

"Father!"

"Lord!"

"Creator!"

"God!"

"Jesus!"

"Love!"

Out of the mouths of children ... And then one little girl of about ten really gives me a surprise.

"Yahweh," she says quietly. I know immediately that this child has been paying attention in church or Sunday School or both.

"Yes! Yes! Yes!" I find myself responding to each reply. "Yahweh!" I repeat in startled wonder when it is pronounced by the girl. I reach down in front of me to pick up the posterboard.

As the children look at what I have written, they look puzzled. "This looks funny, doesn't it?" I ask. They nod.

"Why?" I question.

After a moment's thought, one of the older children says, "There aren't any vowels."

"That's right," I tell her. "The Hebrews didn't use vowels in their writing very often. This is an English translation of the Hebrew letters they used to write 'Yahweh,' the name of God."

"After a while, the name of God became so sacred that the Hebrews wouldn't even pronounce it when they were reading scripture. They would substitute the name 'Adonai' instead. 'Adonai' means 'Lord.'

"Well, what have we learned together this morning?" This is always a risky question with any group, but perhaps particularly with children because they tend to be so honest.

113

"We've learned the name of God," Jerry responds.

"And what is that name?" I ask the group, holding up the posterboard for all of them to see.

"Yahweh!" a number of them reply.

"So, we've learned the Hebrews' name for God was 'Yahweh.' What else have we learned?" An uncomfortable silence follows.

"What if I call you the wrong name or can't remember your name?" I ask.

"Oh, yeah!" Marian says, "I like for you to know my name and not mess it up when you say it."

"And if I did mess it up, what would you do?"

"Tell you how to say it right!" she assures me. And I have no doubt she would.

"Are you telling me your name, your correct name, is important to you?" She nods vigorously.

"In fact, each of your names is important to each of you, right?" I ask the entire group. Numerous little heads bob up-and-down affirmatively.

"Sometimes we get down on ourselves. Sometimes we don't think we're worth much. If that ever happens to you, I hope you'll remember that you are important to God. In fact, you are so important, and God loves you so much, that God knows you by your very own name."

The "Rips"

*"I give you a new commandment, that you love one another.
Just as I have loved you, you also should love one another. By this
everyone will know that you are my disciples, if you have love for
one another."*   — John 13:34-35

Theme: *Anger; tolerance.*

Visual Aid: *Several photographs of a cat.*

———————————

   When the children have gathered on the chancel steps, I ask,
"Do any of you have any pets?" Everyone seems to nod, and since
the group is not overly large this morning, I encourage each of
them to tell me (one at a time) what kind of a pet they have.
   "A cat," says the first child.
   "Ditto," responds the boy next to her.
   "A goldfish," comes the next reply.
   "A cat," says a young man whose family I know, including
their pets.
   "Just one?" I ask, surprised.
   "Well, no, actually three cats," he replies.
   This litany goes on through a few more children, one with a
dog, one with a cat and a dog, and another with a cat.
   "It certainly seems that this group favors cats," I observe. "As
it happens, I have two cats myself, Dylan and Roy. And it's Roy I
want to talk with you about this morning. I've brought a couple of
pictures of him which you may pass around while we talk. As
you'll see, in the pictures he looks rather quiet and calm. I'm sure
most of you have seen cats be quiet and calm — after all, they
sleep nearly eighteen hours every day."
   "Well, Roy is not always as quiet and calm as he looks in those
pictures, even though he's basically shy. Sometimes Roy gets what
my family calls the 'rips.' When a cat gets the 'rips,' it goes racing

around the house after who-knows-what! As far as human eyes can see, the cat isn't chasing anything except its imagination! When Roy gets the 'rips,' he seems to bounce off the walls. The last time this happened was just last week — at 3:30 in the morning. Roy decided that whatever it was he was chasing was in our bedroom. He went racing around the bed ... and over the bed ... and over the people in the bed ... and, obviously, he woke us up.

"At first, I was *very* irritated with him. I thought about getting up, catching him if I could, and really scolding him for his behavior. But then I stopped myself. I realized that wasn't going to do any good. Besides, I had to ask myself, 'Why am I really angry with him anyway?' After all, Roy was just being a cat — and that's what he is. He was just being himself. Nor would I want him to be anything else.'

"By then I was awake, and I found myself wondering if something similar happens when I get angry with a person. You see, it's possible that I'm angry because I have some idea about the way another person ought to be that has nothing to do with who that person really is. Maybe the other person is just being himself

or herself, but because that doesn't match my idea of how the person *should* be, I am angry.

"You know, Jesus taught us that it's important to accept one another just the way we are. That's how he accepts us; that's how he loves us.

"So, you see, I learned something from Roy this week, and I hope you have too. Perhaps the next time you feel angry with someone you'll remember what we talked about today. Then maybe you can take a look at other people and really see them, just as they are. And knowing Jesus loves them that way, maybe you can too. It's important for you to be yourself, who God created you to be; it's important for you to let others be themselves too."

Let Me See Your Shoes!

"Jesus got up from the table, took off his outer robe, and tied a towel around himself. Then he poured water into a basin and began to wash the disciples' feet and to wipe them with the towel that was tied around him." — John 13:4-5

Theme: *Discipleship; tolerance; service.*

Visual Aid: *The children's shoes.*

This morning I greet the children with a question and a request: "Does everyone have shoes on?" They look surprised, as if wondering silently, "Who would come to church without shoes?"

"Let me see your shoes!" I command. Twenty-four little feet emerge from where they have been curled under dresses and slacks, showing off everything from stiff, dressed-up, uncomfortable-looking shoes to a pair of sandals and even a pair of red-and-white striped rubber-soled loafers.

I admire the variety they present, then immediately switch to what must surely seem like a non sequitur when I ask, "Did you know the church has a library?"

Looking puzzled, as if trying to figure out what my question has to do with shoes, a number of children nod affirmatively.

"Did you know it has books in it not just for adults, but also for children?" A couple of children smile now as they nod, obviously remembering books they have read or have had read to them from the church's library.

"Well," I continue, "last Sunday our librarian had a book display in the hall outside the library. I saw a book there that I've thought about for a whole week. It's called *Most Ministers Wear Sneakers.*"[1] The children giggle (along with many adults).

"Why would a minister wear sneakers?" I ask the children. They look very puzzled, as if the idea of sneakers on a minister's feet is just too foreign. So I make the question more personal.

"Maybe it would help to think about why you wear sneakers," I suggest. As their young minds go to work ideas pop out right and left:

"When I play hide-and-go-seek!"

"To play soccer!"

"To play baseball!"

"To walk!"

"To run!"

"Yes, you wear sneakers for all of those reasons," I agree, "and ministers do those things too. For example, they sometimes have a lot of walking to do when they visit folks in the hospitals, and sneakers are more comfortable than other shoes. Sometimes they wear sneakers to play tennis or baseball. Ministers are just like everyone else when it comes to wearing shoes, and one of our ministers is wearing sneakers today. Did any of you know that?"

The children look very surprised as our associate pastor steps forward to show off the tennis shoes on her feet. "She's wearing sneakers today because we're going to be talking about the work camp she and the youth group went to in West Virginia," I explain.

"You know," I continue, "as I thought about ministers wearing sneakers this week, I thought about Jesus and the shoes he wore. Did Jesus wear sneakers?"

Grinning children answer with an emphatic "No!" One child assures me, "He wore sandals."

"That's right," I agree. "Jesus and the disciples wore sandals. The process for getting rubber out of trees hadn't been invented yet, so they couldn't make sneakers. The roads they traveled weren't paved either. So, they walked all those miles together wearing sandals, on dirt roads. Their feet must have gotten pretty dusty. In fact, after a long day's journey, it must have felt pretty good to wash their feet and perhaps even soak them in a bowl of water. That makes me think of the night of the Last Supper when Jesus washed the disciples' feet. Can you imagine Jesus doing that for you?" Some of the children, not yet burdened with low self-esteem, nod affirmatively. "When Jesus washed the disciples' feet he was showing them that it is important to do things for one another. It was one of the many ways Jesus showed the disciples how much he loved them. Through his actions Jesus showed the disciples, and us too, what it means to love one another.

"You may not be asked to wash another person's feet, but I expect you'll be asked to help someone in some way this next week. When you help someone out like that, you're being a minister to them, just as Jesus was to the disciples.

"Let's see a show of hands now. How many of you wear sneakers at least sometimes?" All the children raise a hand.

"And how many of you help out when you're asked to?" All the hands go up again.

"Well, that makes you ministers — ministers who wear sneakers. Maybe you'll remember what we talked about today the next time you put your sneakers on."

---

1. Poling, Nancy Werking, *Most Ministers Wear Sneakers* (New York: Pilgrim Press, 1991).

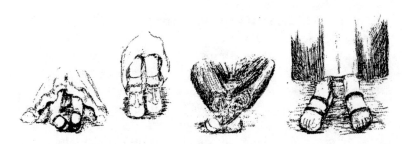

The Treasure Of Christmas

"When they had heard the king, they set out; and there, ahead of them, went the star that they had seen in the East, until it stopped over the place where the child was. When they saw that the star had stopped, they were overwhelmed with joy. On entering the house, they saw the child with Mary his mother; and they knelt down and paid him homage. Then, opening their treasure chests, they offered him gifts of gold, frankincense, and myrrh."
— Matthew 2:9-11

Theme: *Awareness; light; surprises; Christmas.*

Visual Aid: *Two quarters.*

"Have any of you ever found something that surprised you because it was in a place where you didn't expect it to be?" The children think about this question a moment, then a few of them nod affirmatively.

"Well, I have too, several times just recently. The Friday after Thanksgiving I was visiting the Churchill Memorial in Fulton. Walking outside to see the newly acquired section of the Berlin Wall, I noticed something shiny in the grass. When I went to investigate, guess what I found?"

"A dime?" one child asks. I shake my head negatively.

"A quarter?" another suggests.

"Yes," I answer, "in fact, not one, but TWO quarters!" I hold up two quarters. "I was very surprised to find money just lying there in the grass. It was quite an unexpected treasure. Then last Monday, I saw something shiny on the bottom of the swimming pool at the YMCA. Guess what it was?"

"Another quarter!" nearly all of the children respond together.

"No, not a quarter — but a nickel. I had to dive all the way to the bottom — of the deep end! — to see for sure what it was. I was very surprised to find a coin at the bottom of the pool.

"Now I would have missed both of these treasures, the quarters and the nickel, if they hadn't been shiny. But shiny things tend to get our attention. What are some of the shiny things that get your attention at this time of year?"

"Snow!" comes the first gleeful response.

"Yes, snow sparkles when the sunlight hits it," I agree, "and some of you consider it to be quite a treasure, especially when it causes the cancellation of school."

"Ornaments," comes another reply.

"Lights!"

"Icicles!"

Answers begin to erupt from the children right and left. Faintly I hear the suggestion for which I am looking and ask the young man who said it to repeat his idea.

"Stars?" he questions.

"Oh, yes!" I encourage him, "definitely stars. In fact, a very special star nearly 2,000 years ago was so bright and shiny it caused several people to notice it. Who were those people?"

"The wise men!" Somehow I didn't think the kids would have any trouble coming up with that answer.

"And what did they do when they saw the star?"

"They followed it."

"Yes, they followed it. And my, oh my, what a surprise they got when they came to the end of their journey. They were going to find a king! We usually think of kings in palaces and castles, don't we?" The children agree with nods.

"Was this king in a palace?" Vigorously, the children shake their heads.

"Well, where was he?"

"In a stable."

"In a stable? Wow! What a place to find a king, in a stable where animals are kept. But that's where the star led the wise men. And they were wise enough to understand that God could come to us anywhere God chose.

122

"That's still true today. God can surprise us by coming to places we may not be expecting. And sometimes, if we aren't paying attention, we may not notice God. That's one reason it's nice to have shiny ornaments and tinsel and stars as decorations, to remind us to pay attention, to remind us that God can be present with us in unexpected places.

"During this week, whenever something shiny catches your eye, I hope you'll remember that star the wise men saw. They found Jesus when they paid attention, in a place they probably didn't expect to find him. Perhaps you'll remember their story and think of Jesus too when ornaments, tinsel, and stars sparkle into your awareness. For Jesus is the true treasure of Christmas."

Christmas Presence

*"In the beginning was the Word, and the Word was with God,
and the Word was God ... And the Word became flesh and lived
among us, and we have seen his glory, the glory as of a father's
only son, full of grace and truth."*　　　　— John 1:1, 14

Theme: *Memories; God's presence; love; Christmas.*

Visual Aid: *A Christmas tree pin; any present of special significance to the speaker.*

━━━━━━━━━━━━

It is the first Sunday following Christmas. I begin by asking
the children if they enjoyed this special holiday. Faces immediately light up with recent memories of this day which is approached
with such eager anticipation by most children each December.

"Did any of you get any presents?" Every head nods
affirmation.

"Well, don't just sit there so quietly!" This is probably the first
time they've been told that in church. "Tell me about some of your
presents." Hands go up; these kids are so polite!

I nod to one of the boys who says he got a basketball. Then
one of the girls speaks up: "I got this outfit that I'm wearing." All
of us pause to admire her new skirt and sweater. But the children
seem shy this morning. Perhaps they're finding it difficult to focus on any one thing out of an overwhelming abundance. Or perhaps they've not yet lived long enough with their new things to
really own them.

"As I was thinking about this first Sunday after Christmas," I
continue, "it occurred to me that you might want to talk about presents. I started thinking back through the Christmases I have known
and decided to bring a present I got a long time ago." I hold up a
rhinestone pin in the shape of a Christmas tree.

"My dad pinned this to my coat one December day when I was in high school," I tell them. "I thought at the time that it was neat, something to show off to my friends. But now, all these years later, I realize my dad gave me ever so much more than just a pin that day." By this time the children are passing the pin around for a closer look as I continue to speak. Some of them look puzzled, wondering what else my father might have given me.

"You see, the day my dad pinned this little tree to my coat, he gave me a memory. And that is why I still have the pin, because the memory makes it more than just something pretty to wear. Every December I get it out of the special corner of my jewelry box, where I keep it the rest of the year, and pin it to my coat." By now the pin has been returned to me and I demonstrate by pinning it to the lapel of my jacket as I'm talking.

"When I put the pin on, I remember that day my dad gave it to me; I remember my father and how much he loved me. These are good memories, something my dad gave me with the pin.

"All of you got memories with your presents too, though you may not know that yet. When you play with your basketball," I say to the boy who spoke up, "perhaps you'll remember the person who gave it to you." I realize as I am saying this that I am risking that "person" having been Santa Claus — but Santa Claus is worth remembering too.

"And the rest of you, whether your presents were new clothes, toys, games, or books, perhaps you'll remember who gave them to you when you wear the clothes, play with the toys, or read the books. You see, part of a present is the presence of the person who gives it."

"Almost 2,000 years ago all of humanity got the first Christmas present. Does anyone know what that present was?"

"Jesus ..." comes the hushed response, in sort of an awed but certain unison.

"And who gave us such a wonderful present?" I ask.

"God!" some of the older children reply.

"Yes, God. God gave us his son, Jesus. And Jesus never asked much of us in return.

"He did say, 'Follow me.' And he said, 'Remember me.' When we remember him, we still have him with us, we still have the present of his presence, and the presence of God the giver too."

"Why did God give us Jesus?" I ask.

"Because God loves us?" one child questions.

"That's right," I respond. "And that's why folks exchange Christmas presents, because they love one another, and it's a way of remembering God's love for us. Christmas memories are important. They have a way of bringing us closer to God, to Jesus, and to one another."

Anger

"It was the time of the Jewish Passover and Jesus went to Jerusalem where he found in the Temple those who sold oxen, sheep, and doves, and the money-changers. Jesus made a scourge of cords and drove them all out; he overturned the money-changers' tables and coins scattered everywhere. He said, 'This is a house of prayer; you have made it into a den of thieves!' " — John 2:13-16

Theme: *Righteous anger; fairness.*

Visual Aid: *A small cardboard box partially filled with foreign coins.*

After the children gather, I shake the small cardboard box I have brought. The distinctive noise that results cannot be mistaken. "What do you suppose I have in this box?" I ask the children.

"Money!" they answer with an air of excited anticipation.

"Yes, the box contains money," I agree. Then I open it and take out a quarter-sized coin made from copper. I hold it up for everyone to see and ask, "Is this a penny?"

"No," the children respond.

"But it's the same color as a penny," I protest. "Are you sure it's not a penny?"

"It's too big to be a penny," one child says.

"You're right," I tell him. "Perhaps it's a dime. It's got this big number 10 on one side." Again I hold it up for the children, then have them pass it around for a closer look as we continue.

"No, it's too big to be a dime," a girl declares.

"And it's the wrong color," another adds.

"Well, gee," I answer, "do you suppose it's not an American coin at all? Could it be from another country?"

The children agree that it must be since it is not currency any of them recognize.

"Actually," I proceed, "all of the coins in this box are from Hong Kong. It's definitely foreign money. Now, suppose I needed some money to pay my United States income tax. Could I use this money from Hong Kong to do that?"

"No," the children tell me. "You'd have to use American money."

"But what if this was the only money I had?" I probe further. "What could I do then?"

The children think a moment. Then one of them offers, "You might get someone to give you American money for your foreign money."

"That's a good idea!" I respond. "I might trade this money for the same value in U.S. coins.

"The reason I brought foreign money today is because of the story about Jesus' visit to the Temple in Jerusalem at the time of the Jewish Passover. All Jewish men over a certain age had to pay a Temple tax. And just as I would need American money to pay my U.S. income tax, they had to have Jewish money to pay the Temple tax. So, if they came for Passover with foreign money (Greek, or Roman, or Persian, or whatever), they had to exchange it.

"That's why there were people called money-changers in the Temple. They earned their living by exchanging foreign money for Jewish money so people could pay their Temple tax.

"Suppose for a moment that you were money-changers and I came to you with a foreign coin that was worth one dollar. If you only gave me back 95 cents and kept a nickel for yourselves, that would probably be all right with me because I knew you were doing me a favor to exchange my money at all. But, what if you kept more than that? What if you kept 25 cents and only gave me back 75 cents?"

"That wouldn't be fair," several children respond.

"No, it wouldn't be fair," I agree. "I would be charging you more than my services were worth. And that's what happened to the folks who came to the Temple to exchange their money. The money-changers charged them a lot more than was fair. When Jesus saw what was going on, what happened?"

"He got angry and turned over the tables and scattered money all over the place," a boy answers.

"Yes," I reply, "Jesus got angry. And it wasn't just the business with the money-changers that angered him. Back in that time, the Jews practiced animal sacrifice, and the animals used for this had to be absolutely perfect.

"Animals were for sale both inside and outside the Temple. Inside, a pair of doves might cost as much as twenty times what they would cost outside. The problem was that if a person purchased a sacrificial animal outside the Temple, the persons who inspected the animals to be sure they were perfect would almost always find something wrong. Then the person who had bought animals outside would have no choice but to buy more animals inside the Temple — at a much higher price."

"But that wasn't FAIR!" another boy exclaims.

"No, it wasn't fair. And what the money-changers were doing wasn't fair either. That's why Jesus was so angry.

"We don't usually think of anger when we think of Jesus. But sometimes, even he got angry. That day in Jerusalem, he shouted at the people in the Temple, 'This is a house of prayer, and you have turned it into a den of thieves!' He was angry because the people who came to worship were being taken advantage of; he was angry because what the money-changers and animal inspectors were doing was dishonest and unfair.

"Sometimes it is okay to be angry. Sometimes it's even important to be angry. When something is truly wrong and we are moved to action by anger, then anger becomes a good thing. It was Jesus' love for justice and rightness that moved him to anger; it was his compassion and love for the worshipers who were being treated unfairly that caused him to make a whip and drive everyone out.

"All of us get angry at times. Sometimes our anger is good; sometimes it isn't. The only way to tell is to understand the source of our anger. If we are angry just because something didn't go the

129

way we wanted it to or just because we were asked to clean up our room before we went to play, or something like that, then it's something we need to let go of. But if our anger is because someone is being treated unfairly, if it is anger against hatred, or mistreatment, or meanness, then our anger is a good thing. Then it is like the anger Jesus unleashed when he cleared the Temple."

Mending

"Put away from you all bitterness and wrath and anger and wrangling and slander, together with all malice, and be kind to one another, tenderhearted, forgiving one another, as God in Christ has forgiven you. Therefore be imitators of God, as beloved children, and live in love, as Christ loved us and gave himself up for us, a fragrant offering and sacrifice to God."

— Ephesians 4:31—5:2

Theme: *Prayer; love; healing.*

Visual Aid: *A piece of material and a threaded needle.*

As the children gather on the steps of the chancel area in the sanctuary, I pull a piece of red-and-white striped cloth out of my pocket. "What have I brought with me today?" I ask them.

"A piece of material," Deborah replies.

"A piece of material," I repeat as I take one end of it in each hand. I had, prior to the start of worship, cut a tiny slit in one edge of the material to facilitate my forthcoming demonstration.

"What do you suppose will happen if I pull too hard on the ends of this piece of cloth?" I ask.

Several children respond at once:

"It'll rip!"

"You'll tear it!"

"That's right," I agree, "and if I keep on pulling, it will come completely apart, won't it?" As I speak, I tear the cloth in two; it makes a very satisfying sound over the hand-held microphone.

"So, now we have two smaller pieces of material," I continue. "How might I put them back together again?"

"Sew them!" comes an immediate response.

"I could sew them back together, yes," I reply. "How else might I mend the material?"

131

"You could use tape!"

"You might staple it ..."

As I watch their minds work, I wonder if anyone will suggest the ever popular mend-everything-better-than-it-was-before stuff commonly known as super-glue. No one does.

"You can see, when you think about it, that there is more than one way I might put the cloth back together," I continue, "but probably the best way is the first one you suggested, to sew it. That's because cloth is made up of many threads woven together. When we mend it using a needle and thread, we are fixing it with the same stuff it's made of." As I talk, I take a needle and thread from a fold of my robe (where I had hidden it earlier) and begin to sew the two pieces of material back together.

Continuing to sew, I tell the children, "Sometimes things happen to us in life that make us feel like we are going to come apart inside. Sometimes when someone is upset by something, we say the person is really 'torn-up' by what happened. It could be the result of anger, jealousy, or losing someone we care for deeply (a relative, a friend, a pet). There are many circumstances that can cause us to feel 'torn-up' or cause a relationship with someone else to be torn apart. When that happens, what can we use to mend the situation?"

As I watch the children's faces, I know the rest of this sermon is in God's hands; I have no idea what the children will say, and bite my tongue to not make suggestions before they have had time to think about possible replies. How often in a conversation it is important to allow the other person(s) space for silence, relinquishing our need to be in control.

Finally, a tentative response comes: "Prayer?"

"Yes," I answer, with delight, "we can use prayer. Prayer is like the needle that draws the two pieces of cloth back together; prayer can draw two friends back together; prayer can draw us back to God; prayer can heal the hurts inside of us."

"Now, if prayer is like the needle, what do you suppose the thread is that follows prayer?" Once again I watch faces as young imaginations work.

"Happiness?" comes the first response.

132

"Yes, happiness could be one 'thread' that would follow prayer through our lives," I reply. "What else?" The answer I am hoping for is the next to come.

"Love?" The questioning response seems to slide sideways out of the mouth of the shyest child who is sitting at the edge of the group. I look into his eyes and quietly affirm his shy spirit.

"Yes, love is the major thread that follows prayer. And from love we get the threads of understanding, compassion, joy, happiness, and all the other bright threads that keep the pieces of our lives together."

As I hold up my now-completed mending of the previously torn material, I tell the children, "Just as I have mended the cloth with the 'stuff' of which it was made, so too are our relationships and hurt feelings mended with the 'stuff' we're made of — love.

"God is love. God made us in God's own image. Jesus taught us, 'Love one another.'

"The next time you feel angry, jealous, hurt, or somehow torn in two, I hope you will take time to pray about the problem. For it is prayer that can draw the pieces of a relationship, the pieces of our lives, back together again, binding them with the 'thread' we know as love."

A Tale Of Two Trees

"And now faith, hope, and love abide, these three; and the greatest of these is love."   — 1 Corinthians 13:13

Theme: *Jealousy; friendship; love; trust; faith; hope; renewal; self-esteem.*

Visual Aid: *A small cedar tree and some red dogwood leaves.*

———————

As the children gather, I bring over a flowerpot in which I have placed a small cedar tree that "volunteered" in my yard during the summer. I also have red dogwood leaves, hidden in a plastic bag.

After greeting the assembled youngsters, I ask if anyone went outside on Saturday. Most heads nod affirmatively.

"Did anyone notice the trees?" I ask. Several children indicate they did.

"Well, what's happening to them?" I continue.

"They're changing colors!"

"Some of them have turned orange!"

"And red and yellow!"

"Some of them are brown!"

As the children's answers spill over each other, it is obvious that autumn has arrived in all its splendor — and the children have noticed.

"My goodness!" I exclaim. "The trees are putting on their fall colors, aren't they! Have ALL of them changed?"

Several children indicate they have not with a shake of their heads. One little girl points to the tree I have brought and says, "That one won't change. It will stay green."

"That's right," I agree. "It will stay green all year 'round. That's why it is called an EVERgreen tree."

"Well, this morning I have a story for you about a tree just like this one. Once upon a time an evergreen tree was growing up in a big forest beneath the mighty oaks, the tall hickory trees, and alongside the smaller trees like the redbuds and the dogwoods. In fact, this evergreen grew up right next to a dogwood tree.

"The first time the evergreen noticed the dogwood was in the spring. What happens to dogwood trees in the springtime?" I ask the children. They think for a moment.

"Remember," I continue, "it's springtime ..."

"They have flowers!" several children answer.

"Yes; they have flowers. And so did this dogwood tree that was growing next to the evergreen. Well, the evergreen tree looked at how beautiful the dogwood was and caught its breath. 'Oh!' gasped the evergreen in wonder, 'how beautiful you are!'

" 'Why, thank you,' the dogwood replied.

"As the evergreen admired the dogwood, it also became very aware of its own branches, covered just as they always were — in green. It wished it could have such lovely flowers.

"But, as spring faded into summer, the dogwood dropped its flowers and put on green leaves. 'This is better,' the evergreen thought to itself. 'Now I don't feel so out of place. We're both wearing green.'

"But summer, of course, did not last. The days grew shorter, the air grew cooler, and what do you suppose happened to the dogwood tree?"

"Its leaves turned red/orange!" come the almost simultaneous replies.

"Yes," I agree, "its leaves turned red and orange. What about the evergreen tree?"

"It stayed green!" nearly all the children assure me.

"Yes, it stayed green. And once again it was wishing it could be like the dogwood and have pretty red leaves on its branches. It sighed sorrowfully to itself, and the wind picked up the evergreen's sigh and carried it to the dogwood.

"Living next to one another, the evergreen and the dogwood had become good friends. So, when the dogwood heard the evergreen's sad sigh, it decided to help its friend's dream come true. For the dogwood knew it would soon have to let go of its pretty red leaves.

"Patiently the dogwood waited until the wind was just right, blowing toward the evergreen. Then, it let go of its leaves and the wind carried them into the branches of the dogwood's green friend.

" 'Oh my!' the evergreen exclaimed with delight, looking down and admiring all its newly decorated branches. 'How beautiful I am with these wonderful red leaves you have given me! Why, I look like a Christmas tree covered with ornaments!' (You see, the evergreen knew the legend of the forest — that very special evergreens sometimes get picked to become Christmas trees — but that's another story.)

"After a while the evergreen looked up from admiring itself to thank its friend the dogwood and gasped at the dogwood's new appearance! It was BARE! All of its branches were absolutely NAKED! And winter was coming. 'Oh my!' the evergreen exclaimed! 'What will you DO? You're going to be so cold!'

" 'Perhaps I shall just go to sleep,' the dogwood replied and began to yawn. Very soon the first snow came. The evergreen shivered just a little but didn't find winter too terribly cold. It worried though about its bare-branched dogwood friend.

"As the snow built up on the branches of the evergreen it began to feel very strong, supporting all that weight. It also felt very beautiful again, looking down at its deep green branches set off by the sparkling white snow. But even that grew tiresome after a while. The evergreen missed its friend the dogwood.

"Slowly winter passed. Then one day the evergreen noticed bumps on the limbs of the dogwood. The dogwood almost seemed to stretch when its branches bounced in the gentle spring breeze.

"As it awoke, the dogwood felt a little afraid. But then it heard the evergreen singing as the wind sighed through its branches. 'I'm still here!' the song went. 'And I'm still as green as ever. Come on, dogwood; wake up! It's spring!'

"The dogwood found hope and joy in the evergreen's song, struggled awake, and began to open up its beautiful blossoms. The evergreen, who had been lonely while its friend slept, was so very glad to see the dogwood had survived the winter that it wasn't

136

even jealous of the dogwood's spring flowers. It was simply filled with gratitude that this friend who had shared its beauty with the evergreen in the fall was waking up.

"And the evergreen realized that even though the dogwood looked very pretty sometimes, it wasn't necessarily any better to be a dogwood than to be an evergreen; it was just different. The evergreen also knew that it was happy just to be itself, there in the forest, growing with its friend.

"You know, in some ways people are just like the trees in this story. Sometimes we get jealous of how someone else looks and don't like our own appearance. But when we can let go of those feelings and enjoy just being ourselves, we have a lot to give one another. The dogwood gave the evergreen its red leaves in the fall because it loved its friend. And the evergreen gave the dogwood hope and encouragement with its song when the dogwood was waking up in the spring.

"As you go back to your seats, each of you may take one of these red dogwood leaves to remind you that, like the dogwood and the evergreen, you're really special just the way you are. And, like the trees, you have songs to sing and love to give just because you're you."

Freedom

"The tribune came and asked Paul, 'Tell me, are you a Roman citizen?' And he said, 'Yes.' The tribune answered, 'I obtained this freedom with a great sum of money.' Paul said, 'But I was **born** *free.' "* — Acts 22:27-28

Theme: *Freedom; responsibility; citizenship; Fourth of July.*

Visual Aid: *Red, white, and blue clothing. Other options include a flag, a bunch of red, white, and blue flowers, a piece of patriotic bunting, etc.*

"Does anyone know today's date?" I ask the children who have just gathered on the chancel steps.

"July third," several answer. As part of my preparation to talk with the children this morning, I have dressed in red, white, and blue.

"July third ..." I repeat thoughtfully. "Well then, why do you suppose I have dressed like this?" I ask.

"Because tomorrow is the FourthofJuly," the children answer, making the name of the holiday into one solid word.

"The Fourth of July?" I question. "Why would I dress in red, white, and blue for the Fourth of July?"

"Because they are patriotic colors," the children tell me.

"Oh," I reply. "So you're saying the Fourth of July has something to do with our country. And you're right, of course. It is a day we celebrate something called 'freedom.'

"Over 200 years ago, the people who had settled here in America were subjects of the King of England. The English passed some tax laws that the people in America didn't think were fair. So, the Americans declared their independence, their freedom from England.

138

"Now, the interesting thing about freedom is that it is never just *from* something. It is also *for* something. If the Americans declared their freedom *from* England, what did they declare it *for*?" I ask, hoping some of the children are old enough to have discussed this with their parents or have had it in history at school.

"To rule themselves?" comes a questioning response.

"Yes, the Americans declared their freedom *from* England *for* self-rule. What does it mean to be free?" I ask. "Does it mean you can do anything you want to do?"

Some of the children look puzzled; one starts to nod affirmatively; most of them shake their heads to indicate "No."

"No, being free doesn't mean doing anything you want to do," I continue. "That would be a mess and make it pretty hard to live with each other. But being free does mean having a voice in what happens and having some choice about our actions.

"Even in the United States of America everyone has not always been free. Our country fought a Civil War in the mid-1800s and one of the issues that caused the war was slavery. In the end, slavery was abolished in this country.

"God created us to be free creatures and gave us the freedom to choose our actions and our responses to one another and to God. We've talked about that before — that if we did not have the freedom to choose to love God, if God *made* us give our love, then it would not mean anything. But God risked giving us freedom.

"Now, sometimes we make choices that are not good. They may seem good, but when they end up making us angry with one another or hurting one another, they cause separation from one another — and from God too. And that is what we call sin.

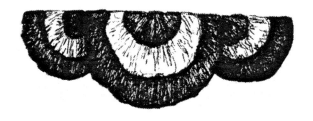

139

"But God cares about us so much that God didn't just leave us to our mistakes. Instead, God sent us Jesus to show us how to live and to save us from our enslavement to sin. Jesus set us free *from* the power of sin *for* life and the freedom to choose to return God's incredible, steadfast, eternal love. Tomorrow, on the Fourth of July, as we celebrate our country's freedom, I hope that you will think about what it means to be free, to have the right to choose, and remember that you were *born* free as children of a loving God who cares for us so much that, for God, giving us freedom is worth every risk.

Happy Birthday!

"When the day of Pentecost had come, they were all together in one place. And suddenly from heaven there came a sound like the rush of a violent wind, and it filled the entire house where they were sitting." — Acts 2:1-2

Theme: *Pentecost; Holy Spirit.*

Visual Aid: *An uninflated red balloon.*

———————

"Did any of you notice anything unusual outside the sanctuary this morning?"

"There were decorations ... streamers ... balloons!" These are the sorts of things near and dear to a child's heart, and indeed they had noticed.

"My goodness!" I exclaim in mock surprise. "It sounds like someone has decorated for a party! Does anyone know why we would be having a party today?" This question stumps them, so I continue.

"Today is a special day in the church. It is called 'Pentecost.' " To get them used to this word that even the older children have heard only a few times in their lives, I ask them to say it with me.

"Pentecost ... So now you're probably wondering what Pentecost means. It's obvious from the decorations in the lobby that it must be an occasion for a party. Why do people have parties?"

"To celebrate something!"

"That's one reason. What sorts of things do you celebrate with a party?"

"Graduation!" comes the firm response from a child with older siblings.

"Yes. And the graduation of our seniors is one of the things we are celebrating in our church today. But what is another reason

141

you have a party — what is a reason every one of you has had a party or been to a party?"

"Birthdays!" several children answer.

"Yes, birthdays. And that's what Pentecost is; it's the birthday of the church. It comes from a Greek word that means the 'fiftieth day.' Pentecost falls fifty days after Easter and it is the day on which the Holy Spirit came to the first Christians. That was the beginning of the church, so on Pentecost, the fiftieth day after Easter, we celebrate the church's birthday.

"Well, since we're going to have a birthday party after worship, maybe we need a balloon to add to our decorations." With this suggestion, I pull a balloon out of my pocket.

"What does this balloon need?" I ask the children.

"Air!" they tell me.

"Ah yes, air. It's not much to look at all flat like this. It's lifeless, isn't it? You know, the Hebrew word *ruach* and the Greek word *pneuma* both have two meanings. Both of them can mean either 'wind' or 'spirit.' So, if I use my wind to blow into this balloon, it will be full of wind, but we could also think of it as full of spirit — something more than itself that keeps it from being flat and lifeless.

"I brought this balloon to help us understand what it meant when the Holy Spirit came to the first Christians. There was a great sound of wind and tongues of fire — which is why I chose a red balloon and why our pastors have red stoles this morning. The Holy Spirit breathed spirit — new life — into that group of Christians and the church was born. Now, what if this balloon didn't have an opening in it for me to blow into?"

"Then you couldn't blow any air in. It would stay flat," the children answer.

"That's right. And just as this balloon needs an opening for air, we need to have an opening for the Holy Spirit to enter us. We create that openness by coming to worship, by praying, by being aware of God, by asking God to fill us with the Holy Spirit. And, filled with the Spirit, we have new life because it makes us live differently. It's like the difference between a flat, lifeless balloon and one filled up for celebration.

"Will you pray with me before you go? God, thank you for the gift of the Holy Spirit which connects us to you and fills us with your love just as surely as we are able to fill balloons with our wind. We praise you, God, and offer our thanksgiving for the gift of the church on this day of Pentecost. In Jesus' name we lift our prayer to you. Amen."

"Put Yourself In My Shoes!"

"To the weak I became weak, so that I might win the weak. I have become all things to all people, that I might by all means save some."
— 1 Corinthians 9:22

Theme: *Understanding; compassion; incarnation; discipleship.*

Visual Aids: *A pair of new shoes.*

"Have any of you ever had a new pair of shoes?" The children greet this question with looks of surprise, as if to say, "Who hasn't? Of course we have."

As I look around the group, I continue: "Probably all of you have had new shoes. In fact, you've had new shoes a number of times because you are all growing, probably faster than you can wear shoes out. I have new shoes too, new shoes I haven't even worn yet except to try them on." With these words I take a pair of new shoes out of a shopping bag.

"There they are, my new shoes — my BIG new shoes. None of your feet are this big yet, but some day they may be — or even bigger!

"You can tell these shoes are brand-new because they aren't scuffed like the older ones I'm wearing. The soles still have tread on them too; the shoes I'm wearing nearly have the tread worn off." I hold one foot up so the children can inspect the bottom of one of my current shoes and compare it with the soles of my new ones.

"You know, shoes are very personal. Sometimes you can recognize other people just by seeing their shoes. Your shoes go everywhere you go; they take you through the world.

"Thinking about shoes, I was wondering if any of you have ever heard anyone say, 'Well, put yourself in my shoes!' " Several children nod affirmatively.

"What did the person who said that mean?" I question.

"Put yourself in my place," Cynthia replies.

"Why would he want you to do that?" I continue.

"So I can understand how he feels, I guess," Cynthia answers.

"I agree with you," I tell her. "Sometimes the best way to understand how someone else feels or why someone else is acting in a certain way is to try to imagine what it would be like to be in his place, to put ourselves in his shoes. Our youth group will be doing something like that in a few weeks when they conduct a thirty-hour fast. They will have no solid food for thirty hours. They are going to get hungry. But they'll begin to understand, in a way they would not be able to without experiencing hunger themselves, what it is like to not have enough to eat.

"The apostle Paul wrote a letter to the church at Corinth in which he said, 'I have become all things to all people.' He literally tried to experience whatever the people he was with experienced so that he could understand them, and so they — knowing he understood them — might listen to what he had to say about Jesus.

"There's someone who loves us very, very much, who cared enough to put himself in our shoes. Do you know who that is?"

"God," comes the quiet, awed, but unquestioning response.

"Yes," I agree, "God. God came to be with us through his son Jesus. Jesus literally put himself in our place when he suffered and died on the cross.

145

"Because God came to us in Jesus, God knows what it's like to be human. God knows what it's like to laugh, to cry, to be hurt, to dance with joy, to give someone a hug. God knows what it's like to walk in our shoes, because God has done it. And because God knows, because God understands us out of God's own experience, we can go to God with everything that life is. We can rejoice with God when good things happen and take our tears and fears to God when we are hurt or afraid, *certain* that God understands because God has experienced those things too — because God, through Jesus, put himself in our shoes.

"Putting yourself in someone else's shoes means you care enough to try to understand him or her. It is a wonderful way in which to show our love and compassion for others. And when we do, we are following the example set for us by God in Jesus. When we try to understand another person by putting ourselves in his or her shoes, we are being disciples of Christ."

Risking It All

"Now there was a woman who had been suffering from hemorrhages for twelve years. She had endured much under many physicians, and had spent all that she had; and she was no better, but rather grew worse. She had heard about Jesus, and came up behind him in the crowd and touched his cloak, for she said, 'If I but touch his clothes, I will be made well.' Immediately her hemorrhage stopped; and she felt in her body that she was healed of her disease." — Mark 5:25-29

Theme: *Faith.*

Visual Aid: *A picture of a large crowd.* (**National Geographic** *magazine is an excellent source.*)

————————

"What does it mean to take a risk?" I ask the assembled children. As the seconds of their silence lengthen I wonder if today's topic is going to be too ephemeral for their concrete way of thinking. Just as I am about to answer my own question, I hear a soft voice inquire, "Does it mean to do something dangerous?"

"Yes!" I reply. "Taking a risk is often dangerous because taking a risk means that you might lose something that is important to you. But sometimes it is necessary to take a risk in order to gain something that is even more important than what we stand to lose.

"The Bible is full of stories about people who take risks, one of whom was a woman who had been bleeding for twelve years. She had been to all sorts of doctors looking for a cure. In fact, she had spent all her money paying them to treat her. But nothing helped.

"Then she heard about Jesus, and she *knew* that if she could get near enough to him just to touch his robe she would finally be well. But there was a BIG problem.

"You see, the condition from which she suffered made her an outcast in the society in which she lived, because a person who was bleeding was thought to be 'unclean.' That meant she was not allowed to touch any other person — and no one else could touch her.

"Can you imagine what that would have been like? For twelve long years not even her own family had so much as given her a hug. It was as if she didn't exist. It must have been just awful. Why, twelve years is longer than any of you have been alive!"

By now the children are wide-eyed with attention. They know they would not like to have to do without hugs.

"Still, the woman knew she at least had to touch Jesus' robe if she was going to get well. But there was another problem. Jesus had gotten pretty famous and wherever he went, there was usually a big crowd. It may have looked something like this crowd." I hold up an aerial photograph of 8,000 people gathered for the Boston Marathon.

"Now, just imagine that Jesus is right in the middle of all these people. Would it be easy to get to him?"

"Noooo!" the children answer.

"Would it be possible to get to him without touching anyone else?"

"Probably not," several children reply.

"No, probably not," I agree. "So, you see what a big risk this woman was taking. She wasn't supposed to touch ANYONE, and yet she was going to worm her way through a huge crowd of people and try to get close enough to Jesus at least to touch his robe. Why, if anyone realized who she was and what she was doing she might have been killed! She was taking a really big risk!

"But the risk was worth it, because for her life wasn't worth continuing the way it was. So, she went out to the countryside where Jesus was walking down the road in the middle of all these people. And she managed finally to get close enough just to touch the hem of his robe. Instantly, she felt his power flow through her, and she knew she had been healed.

"However ... Jesus felt the power flow out of him! He knew someone had touched him. In fact, he turned to the disciples and asked, 'Who touched me?'

"Well, they almost laughed at him for asking such a thing. 'Hey!' they said to him. 'Look around yourself. You're in the middle of a huge bunch of people. How are we supposed to figure out who touched you? It could have been anyone.'

"But the woman had heard Jesus' question too. So then, even though she knew people would probably recognize her as the 'unclean' one and she might get in all sorts of trouble, she told Jesus she was the one who had touched his robe.

"And do you know what Jesus did?" The children just shake their heads, waiting expectantly for me to continue. "Jesus wasn't at all angry. He said to her, gently, 'Daughter, your faith has made you whole. Go in peace and be healed of your disease.'

"You know, sometimes our faith requires us to take a risk too. And when it does, it helps to remember that even God takes risks. God takes an enormous risk by giving us the freedom to choose what we will do, how we will act, whom we will love. God wants our love, but God will not force us to give it. If God did, then it wouldn't be of any value to God. So God takes a risk on us, giving us life and the freedom to choose how we will live it. But God finds the risk worth taking — because the possibility that we will risk returning God's love is worth it. God risks everything on us in the hope that we will risk everything on God."

Attitudes

"For everything there is a season, and a time for every matter under heaven."   — Ecclesiastes 3:1

Theme: *Attitudes; time; control; New Year's Day.*

Visual Aid: *A brown paper sack in which I have placed several different styles of calendars, an egg timer, a mechanical timer, and an alarm clock.*

Whether by serendipity or grace (if, in fact, there is a difference), light snow during the night has conveniently set the stage for my talk with the children. I begin with an imagined conversation:

" 'There's just not enough of it,' Sarah wailed to her brother and sisters.

" 'It's melting away!' Mary cried with distress.

" 'It IS going much too fast,' Jason agreed.

" 'I don't think it's going fast enough,' Sally objected.

"Just then, their mother stepped to the door and said, 'Come in for supper, children. It will be gone before you know it.'

"What," I ask the assembled children, "do you think Sarah and the others were talking about?"

Almost before there is time to blink, several of the children say, "Snow!" Obviously, this answer is not unexpected, aided by the overnight gift with which Mother Nature blanketed the ground.

"Yes," I agree, "they could have been talking about snow. But, they weren't. Is there anything else that sometimes seems to melt away, something that sometimes is not enough for some folks and too much for others? Is there anything else that goes too fast for some people and too slowly for others?"

The children think for a moment. Then with a triumphant look Jeff exclaims, "Time!"

"You guessed it, Jeff," I continue. "That's what these children were talking about. And it seems like an appropriate thing to discuss here at the beginning of a brand-new year. What are some of the ways in which we measure time?"

"With a watch," Beth offers. I agree, noting that I have a watch on my wrist, then ask for other ideas.

"A clock," Brad says. I pull an alarm clock out of the big shopping bag I've brought and set it on the floor in front of the children. "What else?" I question.

"One of those sand things," Carol answers.

"Yes," I agree, "and I have one of those in here too." I take out an hourglass egg-timer and set it on the floor by the clock.

"Do you have a sundial in there?" Keith asks with a grin.

"No, I don't," I answer. "But that is a good suggestion. I might have found a picture of one in a catalogue if I'd had time to look for one."

"Daylight," Sarah pronounces, looking around the sanctuary at the windows.

"Yes," I respond, "we can tell what time of day it is by where the sun is in the sky, by which windows it is shining through in here or in your homes. And daylight brings up the issue of days. How do we measure days, weeks, months ..."

"With calendars!" several children simultaneously respond before I ever get to "years." Now I begin pulling calendars out of my bag — wall calendars, desk calendars, pocket calendars.

"These come in many different shapes and sizes and can be found with subjects from sports to angels, cartoons to quotations," I tell the children. "We seem to be very conscious of time in our lives, don't we? Just look at all these things we have to help us keep track of time. It's almost as if by keeping track of it we have a sense that we can somehow control time. But we really can't. Time is not in our hands; it's in God's.

"We are not in control of our time. We are not in control of our lives. God is. But we are in control of our attitudes. And, if you think back to the story we began with, that was the difference between Sally and her brother and sisters. Sally thought time was going much too slowly. The others thought it was getting away from them, going too fast. The difference was their attitude.

"We really do have a choice about our attitude. We can *choose* to be happy or sad. We can *choose* to be angry or forgiving. We can *choose* to hate or to love. God gives us the power and the freedom of choice. How we experience our time, how we experience our lives, is largely dependent on our choice of attitude.

"Our time is in God's hands. Our lives are in God's hands. But our attitudes are up to us. Sometimes it is difficult not to be sad or angry or unhappy. Sometimes it seems like nothing is going right. When we are in those times, it is especially important to remember who really is in charge, to remember that God is present in absolutely every moment of our lives. For God, 'there is a time for every matter under heaven.' "

Children Of God

"See what love the Father has given us, that we should be called children of God; and that is what we are." — 1 John 3:1a

Theme: *Love; children; parents; God.*

Visual Aid: *The children themselves.*

"I asked all of you to come up here for the children's sermon — so I guess all of you are children, right?" The youngsters readily agree.

"Am I a child?" I continue.

"No!" comes the immediate response.

"Well, then, perhaps I don't belong up here. Maybe I'd better leave ..." As I begin to get up, I get a thoughtful expression, and stop in mid-motion.

"No, wait a minute," I say to the children, "I'd like to talk about this first. I think I AM somebody's child. My mom and my dad will always be my mom and my dad no matter how big or how old I become. I'm their child, no matter what. So, maybe I'll just stay here with you after all."

As I settle back down, I ask, "What does it mean to be somebody's child?"

"You have someone to call Mom and Dad," Susan suggests.

"That's right," I agree. "What else?" As I pause, the children are silent, so I prompt them with an additional question: "Do your parents ever expect you to do anything?"

"Oh yes!" the children answer.

"Like what?" I ask.

"Clean my room," Brian says with a look of distaste.

"What else?"

"Clean the dishes!"

"Do my chores!"

153

"Do the laundry!"

"Do the laundry?" I repeat in questioning surprise. "Gee, I like that one. Maybe I should have had children!" Laughter ripples through the sanctuary with my words.

"Take care of pets!"

"Mow the lawn!"

"Gosh!" I say in mock surprise. "You guys are useful! Well, it seems to me that parents also do something for you. What might that be?"

"They take care of me," Robert answers.

"Why do they do that?" I ask him.

"Because they love me," he says.

"Yes, because you are their child. And we have learned this morning that we are all children of someone. We all have parents who gave us life. And we are all children of someone else too. When we say 'The Lord's Prayer,' how does it begin?"

"Our Father ..." little voices reply, trailing off.

"Yes, it begins 'Our Father ...' So, that makes us children of ..."

"Of the Lord!" the children answer.

I realize I am on the point of confusing their theology, so I say, "The Lord Jesus taught us this prayer. That is why we call it 'The Lord's Prayer.' But to whom do we pray this prayer? Who is it we address when we say, 'Our Father...?' "

"God?" one small voice questions.

"Yes," I answer, "God. We are all children of God. In fact, everyone in this room is qualified to come up here for the children's sermon because everyone here is a child of God. And that's why God loves us, because we are God's children. This week, I'd like you to think about how much God loves you and what you might do during the week to show your love for God."

Connections

"But God, who is rich in mercy, out of the great love with which he loved us even when we were dead through our trespasses, made us alive together with Christ — by grace you have been saved."
— Ephesians 2:4-5

Theme: *God, the giver of life; Holy Spirit; separation from God and one another; connecting with God and one another.*

Visual Aid: *A tree root, an electrical extension cord, and a telephone (NOT a "cordless" phone).*

───────────

As the children watch, I reach into the bag I've brought and pull out a gnarled tree root. "What is this?" I begin. Not unexpectedly, several children tell me it is a stick.

"It does look like a stick," I agree, "but there is another name for this particular part of a tree."

"A branch?" Charles asks.

"No, but you're closer. Move farther down the tree," I suggest.

"The trunk?" Timothy questions, a bit mystified. At this point a part of my mind wanders to an apparent lack of botanical education among these children as I tell them, "It's a root."

"Oh, the bottom!" Timothy interjects triumphantly.

"That's right, Tim; the bottom of the tree. What does the root do?"

"The tree uses it to get minerals and water," Brian answers.

"Yes," I agree as I reach into the bag once more. This time I pull out an extension cord.

"Now, what's this?" I ask.

"An electric cord!" Jennifer offers.

"Okay," I respond. "It's an electric cord. So, what would I use it for?"

"To bring electricity to something, like a lamp," Christopher replies.

"Yes," I answer. "Now, what's this?" I ask, pulling one more item out of my bag.

"It's a TELEPHONE!" comes the unanimous response.

"Ah, a telephone ...You all knew that one right away! How many of you have ever used a telephone?" I question. Every child present raises a hand.

"Oh good," I continue. "Now suppose I wanted to make a call on this telephone. Could I do that?"

"NO!" comes another unanimous response.

"Why not?" I ask.

"Because it isn't connected," Nancy answers.

"Oh, so it has to be connected before it will work?" I question.

"Yes," Nancy and several others affirm.

"So if I pick up the receiver and listen for a dial tone, there won't be one, right?" I do exactly what I have described. "Sure enough, it's dead; no dial tone.

"What if I had a lamp connected to this cord but pulled the plug out of the wall socket? Would I be able to turn the lamp on?"

"No," the children answer. "It's got to be plugged in," Christopher assures me.

"Well, let's go back to this tree root for a moment," I suggest. "It isn't doing the tree much good, is it?" Several children shake their heads in a negative response.

"It's not connected to the tree anymore," Jennifer observes.

"That's right, Jennifer. What happens to a tree without roots?" I ask.

"It will die," Jennifer answers.

"Yes, it will die; it will die if it is disconnected, cut off from its roots. And if the plug is disconnected, cut off from the wall socket, the cord will have no power. And if the telephone is disconnected, cut off from its cord, it will not work; it will be 'dead.'

"By now all of you may be wondering just what this has to do with you or anything else. But you see, just like the root, the cord, and the phone, we all need to be connected to something to feel alive. What is our source of life?" I ask this, fully cognizant of the risk I'm taking.

"God?" Simon questions.

"Yes, God. It is God who created us and God who gives us life. But, sometimes we don't feel very alive; sometimes, we feel dead inside. Sometimes we feel cut off from one another and from God. For example, if I were angry with you, Simon, I might decide not to speak to you. I would be cutting myself off from you.

"When we separate ourselves from each other due to anger or jealousy or hatred, we are also separating ourselves from God. It has the same effect on our spirit that cutting the root off the tree has on the tree, or unplugging the cord has on the lamp, or disconnecting the cord has on the phone. When we cut ourselves off like that we feel lifeless.

"But you see, God doesn't like being cut off from us. So God sent us Jesus, to reconnect with us. God does that by giving us the Holy Spirit through Jesus. Like electricity, the Spirit is not something you can see. But you can feel it within you — feelings expressed as joy, peace, kindness, and love. These are the fruits of the Spirit, and they are just the opposite of the feelings we have

when we are disconnected. The Holy Spirit connects us all to each other and to God through Jesus Christ.

"Connected, we feel alive; disconnected, we feel lifeless — dead inside. When we are mean to other people, or in some other way fail to live the example Jesus set for us, we sin. And that makes us feel dead inside.

"But God, who loves us even when we are dead from our trespasses, makes us alive, together, through Jesus. Jesus connects us to God and to each other."

Getting Ready

"As it is written in the book of the words of the prophet Isaiah, 'Prepare the way of the Lord, make his paths straight. Every valley shall be filled, and every mountain and hill shall be made low; and the crooked shall be made straight, and the rough ways made smooth.'"
— Luke 3:4-5

Theme: *Advent; waiting; preparation; making room for Jesus.*

Visual Aid: *A broom.*

Having invited the children to come to the front of the sanctuary, I turn to the steps leading into the chancel area and begin to sweep, using the broom I have brought for this purpose. As the children arrive, I move to one side so they can take their places on the steps.

"What was I doing as you walked up here?" I begin.

"Sweeping," they answer.

"Why was I doing that?" I continue.

"To get the floors clean," comes their response.

"That's right," I affirm. "I was sweeping away some of the straw that has fallen out of the manger, so you wouldn't have to sit on it. I was *preparing* the steps for your coming."

Then, changing my line of thought in order to keep their attention, I ask, "Have any of you ever cleaned a carpet?" I am surprised at the number of hands which go up, indicating which children have done so.

"Wow! What a bunch of helpers you must be at home!" I tell them. Then I ask, "Well, when you clean a carpet, do you normally use a broom?"

"No, a vacuum cleaner," comes a virtually unanimous reply.

"Ah, yes, a vacuum cleaner ... that *would* be a better tool to use on a carpet than a broom."

"We are presently in a season of the church year which we call 'Advent,'" I continue, again with an abrupt change of subject to keep their attention from wandering. "You may be asking yourselves, 'What has Advent got to do with sweeping the floor?' My answer to that would be that both of them have to do with preparation. Who knows what it means to prepare?"

Jason answers, "To get ready."

"Yes," I agree, " 'to prepare' means 'to get ready.' When I was sweeping the floor, I was getting ready for you to come sit here on these steps. And Advent involves getting ready for someone too. For whom are we waiting?"

"For Jesus," several children breathe the name together, with soft reverence. Impressed by their hushed expectancy, I decrease the volume of my own voice as I respond.

"Yes, we are waiting for Jesus. And, as we would for any guest who is important to us, we need to prepare for his coming. This doesn't necessarily involve sweeping the floor, but it could. What are some of the ways in which we get ready for Jesus in our lives? How do we make the way into our lives clear for him?"

"With prayer?" Jimmy questions.

"Yes," I agree. "What else?"

"Doing nice things for other people."

"Thinking of others."

"Reading the Bible."

"Lighting the Advent candles."

Their responses come with increasing speed as the thoughts of one child engender another's. Finally, as their ideas dwindle, I suggest, "I can think of one more. What were we doing just before you came up here?"

"Singing!" they answer.

"Yes, we were singing; music can be a very important part of our getting ready to receive Jesus into our lives, into our hearts. All of the things you have listed are the right 'tools' for the job, just as a vacuum cleaner is the right tool for the job of cleaning the carpet.

"Jesus will not come storming into anyone's life as an uninvited guest; but he will come into the life of everyone who invites

161

him. And if we invite him into our lives, we need to prepare the way for him; we need to open our hearts to receive him.

"You know, it's a funny thing about an open heart. It can't hang onto anger, or hatred, or jealousy, or any of that stuff. Those things just fall right on out of an open heart, and when they do, there is a whole lot more room for us to receive Jesus and his love.

"Will you pray with me before you go?" As the children and I bow our heads, I offer this prayer: "God, we are here together in this Advent time, this waiting time — and sometimes it's very hard to wait. So help us, God, to use this time to prepare, to get ready for Jesus, to open our hearts, to let go of the stuff that stands in his way. Help us to make room in our hearts, room in our often too-busy lives, room to let the Christ Child in. It is in the name of Jesus, the one for whom we prepare, that we offer our prayer. Amen."

Only The Messiah

"Jesus went on with his disciples to the villages of Caesarea Philippi; and on the way he asked his disciples, 'Who do people say that I am?' And they answered, 'John the Baptist; and others, Elijah; and still others, one of the prophets.' He asked them, 'But who do you say that I am?' Peter answered him, 'You are the Messiah.' "
— Mark 8:27-29

Theme: *Love; friendship; discipleship; revelation.*

Visual Aid: *A wooden heart.*

———————————

As the children settle down on the chancel steps, I welcome them, then open my palm to reveal a small wooden heart. "Can anyone tell me what this is?" I inquire.

"It's a heart!" several youngsters answer together.

"Yes, it's a heart. Does it make you think of anything in particular?" I ask.

"Valentine's Day!" David responds with a triumphant grin.

"Love ..." comes another, more tentative, almost wistful reply from Marcia.

"Anything else?" I ask, just to be sure everyone who wants to say something has an opportunity.

"They already took all the good ones!" pouts Robert.

"It makes me think of Jesus," says Jimmy.

This causes Robert to roll his eyes as if to say, "I wish I'd thought of that."

"Valentine's Day ... Love ... Jesus ..." I reiterate, picking up the threads the children have offered. "I think these all have to do with friendship. You know, Jesus had some very close friends, his disciples. One day when they were out walking together, Jesus asked them, 'Who do people say that I am?'

163

"Well, of course, the disciples had been asking themselves this very question as they had gotten to know Jesus better. They realized he was a special guy. 'Some people say you are John the Baptist,' they told him. 'Some say you are Elijah, and others, one of the prophets.'

"Then Jesus asked them, 'But who do you say that I am?' Peter answered Jesus. Do any of you know what Peter said?"

"Didn't he tell Jesus he was the Son of God?" Rebecca inquires.

"Yes, he did. Peter said to Jesus, 'You are the Messiah!' Now that was quite a thing for Peter to say. I mean, it was a pretty bold statement, and he might have been wrong. But, of course, he was right. What I'm wondering is how did Peter KNOW that Jesus was the Messiah?"

The children think about this for a moment. To help them out, I remind them that the disciples had been traveling with Jesus for several years.

"They saw him do miracles ..." John says.

"Yes, they did," I agree, "and that certainly revealed the power of God. Do you think that's how Peter knew?"

"His heart told him!"

David's statement hangs in the air for a moment like a brilliant star. Then I ask, "What do you mean by that, David?"

"I mean Peter knew in his heart that Jesus was the Messiah."

"That's right, David. And Peter knew that because Jesus was his dearest friend and because Peter had the courage to listen to what his heart said. Peter had been with Jesus and had seen how Jesus treated other people. He had seen the unconditional nature of the love Jesus offered to the sick, to the poor, to social outcasts, to tax collectors and sinners; he had seen how Jesus accepted people he met just as they were — and offered them his friendship, his love. Peter had seen all this and had received the gift of Jesus' love himself. And in return, Peter's heart was filled with love for his friend. His heart told him only the Messiah could so love the world.

"You know, we still meet Jesus in our world. Whenever we help someone who needs assistance, when we offer food to someone who is hungry, when we visit people who are sick or in some sort of trouble and offer them our love and support, we are bringing the presence of Jesus to them through our action. And whenever we receive such blessing from another, when we are the one who is fed, or visited, or given the help we require, then we meet Jesus in that person, see him in her eyes, feel his touch through her hand, know his presence through her gift of love.

"Jesus asked the disciples, 'Who do you say that I am?' And that is a question he asks all of us every day of our lives. It is a question we answer by our actions. There is a song about that. It asks us to walk hand-in-hand with each other — to show our love for each other — so people will know we are Christians, by our love for one another.[1]

"Do any of you know that song?" I continue. Most of the children nod affirmation so I ask them and the congregation to sing it with me. After the song, I add this thought: "They'll know we are Christians by our love ... That's how the world will know we are Christians. That's how the world knows Jesus Christ. That's how Peter knew who Jesus was, by his love."

---

1. "They'll Know We Are Christians," 1996, FEL Publications, assigned to the Lorenz Corp., Dayton, Ohio.

Help Wanted

" 'Who gives speech to mortals? Who makes them mute or deaf, seeing or blind? Is it not I, the LORD? Now go, and I will be with your mouth and teach you what you are to speak.' But he said, 'O, my Lord, please send someone else.' "   — Exodus 4:11-13

Theme: *Discipleship; trust; courage.*

Visual Aid: *The "want ad" section of the newspaper.*

"Have any of you ever gone to look for a job?" I ask the assembled children. My question brings looks of surprise to their faces, along with soft chuckles from the congregation.

"Probably none of you is old enough yet to have gone job hunting," I continue. "But I was looking through the 'Help Wanted' advertisements in the newspaper the other day and decided to circle all the jobs that said, 'Experience required.' " I hold up the results of my work; the children note that nearly everything on the two exposed pages is circled.

"Looking at this, I realized that most available jobs require a person who applies to have some experience. That caused me to wonder what sorts of jobs required no experience, and suddenly I thought of Moses. All of you have heard of Moses, haven't you?" The children respond affirmatively to this question which I ask only to keep them involved.

"Well, God had a special job for Moses and used a most unusual means to get Moses' attention. Moses was out herding sheep and God caused a nearby bush to burn — only the bush was not destroyed by the fire. Moses saw the flames and noted the fact that the bush didn't seem to be harmed, so he went to investigate. As he approached the bush, Moses heard a voice say, 'Moses! Moses!'

" 'Here I am,' Moses answered, looking around to see who had called his name.

" 'Moses!' the voice went on, 'take off your shoes, for the ground on which you are standing is holy.' Probably Moses couldn't get his shoes off fast enough, still wondering who was speaking to him.

"Then the voice said, 'I am the God of your ancestors, the God of Abraham, Isaac, and Jacob.'

"Immediately, Moses turned his face away from the burning bush because he was afraid to look at God. Then God told Moses that he was to go to Egypt to tell Pharaoh to set the Israelites free from their bondage, and that Moses should then lead the Israelites out of Egypt.

"Well, you can just imagine how Moses must have felt. God was asking a simple sheepherder to go tell a king what to do! So Moses asked, 'Who am I that I should go and do this?' And God told Moses not to worry about that, saying, 'I will be with you.'

"Moses thought about this for a moment, then said, 'But what if the Israelites ask me your name?'

" 'My name is Yahweh,' God answered. 'I am the God of your ancestors, Abraham, Isaac, and Jacob, and this shall be my name forever.'

" 'Well,' Moses objected again, 'what if they still tell me I did not speak to God?'

"So God asked Moses, 'What is that in your hand?'

" 'It is a staff,' Moses answered. A staff was a very long stick shepherds used in their work.

" 'Throw your staff on the ground,' God commanded Moses.

"So Moses did, and immediately the staff turned into an enormous snake! Needless to say, Moses backed away from it. But then God told Moses to grab the snake by its tail — and Moses DID, which had to take a lot of courage as big as that snake must have been. When Moses touched the snake's tail, it immediately turned back into a shepherd's staff. God showed Moses how to do a couple of other miraculous things too so he'd have plenty of proof that it was God he'd been talking to.

"But Moses still did not want to do what God asked. After all, Pharaoh was the ruler of Egypt and Moses really didn't want to have to go tell Pharaoh that he'd have to let all his slaves go free because the God of the Hebrew people said so.

"So, Moses said, 'God, I really can't do this for you; I just don't speak well enough to do what you want me to do.' But God told Moses not to worry about having the right words. 'I will be with you and will put the words in your mouth,' God said.

"However, even that did not convince Moses. 'Please,' he said to God, 'send someone else.'

"God's patience ran out with that. It was the fifth time Moses had tried to get out of the work God had in mind for him. God told Moses, 'Your brother Aaron is a good speaker. You may take him with you, and I will give you both the words to say, but you WILL do this. Now go. Your brother is already coming to meet you.' So, finally, Moses did as God asked.

"Now in hearing this story, you might wonder that anyone would say no to God, especially FIVE times. But I think Moses did so because he was afraid to do what God asked of him; he had no experience and he didn't feel as if he could do the job. At times all of us are asked to do things that seem impossible. It may be our parents who ask, or a teacher, or even God. Rather than saying, 'I can't do this,' I think it is important to try, to do the best that we can, and to trust — just as Moses finally had to trust — that God will be there to help us do what needs to be done."

Letting Go

"... do not let the sun go down on your anger ... Put away from you all bitterness and wrath and anger and wrangling and slander, together with all malice, and be kind to one another, tenderhearted, forgiving one another, as God in Christ has forgiven you."
— Ephesians 4:26b, 31-32

Theme: *Forgiveness; anger; risk; tension.*

Visual Aid: *Several large rubber bands.*

As the children gather in the front of the sanctuary, I extract a large rubber band from my pocket. I dangle it from my index finger and ask one of the closer children to hook a finger through the other end. Once she has done so, I gently begin to pull the rubber band taut. Just as I am about to explain the concept of tension, the rubber band snaps! It is always wise to be prepared for surprises (Divine intervention?) during the children's sermon; I reach in my pocket for another rubber band and reconnect with a now cautious child who will only allow a minimum of tension to be placed on this one.

"The stress Lucy and I are putting on this rubber band," I explain to the children, "is what we call tension. You have already seen what happens if the tension is too great."

"Yeah," Alan agrees. "The rubber band breaks!" Lucy winces noticeably with this pronouncement.

"In some ways," I continue, "our lives are like this rubber band. Many situations and relationships tug us in many different directions. Tension builds up. And if there is too much tension, what happens?"

"We break?" Jean Paul asks tentatively.

"Yes," I answer, "we break — maybe not on the outside where other people can see it, but we feel snapped-in-two inside. Outward

169

expressions of too much tension inside of us include things like tears and anger.

"Now suppose I wanted to loosen the tension on this rubber band," I suggest. "What would I need to do?" "Let go of it," several children respond. Another anxious look passes across Lucy's face as she leans toward me in case I follow this suggestion.

"Yes," I answer, "to loosen the tension, one or both of us would have to let go of the rubber band. But if I just let go of my end, what's going to happen to Lucy?" I ask.

"Her fingers will get popped!" comes a very certain reply.

"So what do I need to do to be sure Lucy doesn't get hurt?" I ask.

"Let go slowly," one child answers.

"Yes, I must let go, slowly and gently, easing off on the tension we have created between us. Now, suppose that instead of a rubber band, there was the tension of anger between us. What would I need to do to get rid of that tension?"

"Let go of it?" a child asks.

"Let go of what?" I respond.

"Your anger?" he guesses.

"Yes; I would need to let go of my anger. I would need to forgive Lucy for whatever I thought she had done to cause my anger. I would need to speak kind, gentle words to her, to let her know I had let go of my anger, to ease the tension.

"When Saint Paul wrote to the folks in a place called Ephesus, one of the things he said in his letter was, 'Don't let the sun go down on your anger.' What do you think he meant by that?"

This proves to be too much for their young minds to grasp, so I ask another question. "What happens when the sun goes down?"

"It gets dark," the children tell me.

"And what do you do when it gets dark?" I continue.

"Go to bed," many of them answer.

"So, when Saint Paul says, 'Don't let the sun go down on your anger,' he's saying if you are angry, let go of it right away. Don't let your anger hang on day after day. Don't go to bed without forgiving the person you are angry with or letting go of the situation that you have reacted to with anger.

170

"You've all seen what happens to a rubber band when too much tension is put on it. The same thing happens to people when they let tension build up. We all get angry sometimes. But it is very important to learn to let go of that anger and not let it break us up inside."

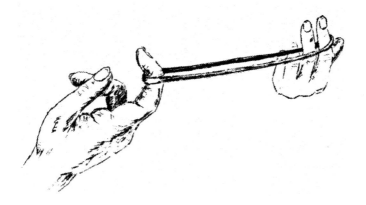

Grapes And Donuts

"I am the living bread that came down from heaven. Whoever eats of this bread will live forever." — John 6:51a

Theme: *Communion; friendship; love.*

Visual Aid: *A picnic basket containing a tablecloth, paper napkins, grapes, donuts, a plate, and a bowl.*

As the children gather I place a rectangular basket on the floor. To begin our discussion, I ask, "What kind of basket is this?" Knowing children are very concrete, literal thinkers, I am not surprised by their initial response: "It's a woven basket."

"Yes, it is woven," I agree.

Then, in an effort to get them to think about what its use might be, I ask, "What do you suppose I have inside the basket?" As their silence stretches beyond my comfort zone I prod, "Any guesses?" No one answers, so I open the lid.

"It's a picnic!" several children announce as they see dishes and a red-and-white checked tablecloth.

"Yes, it's a picnic," I affirm, "and this is a picnic basket. I thought you might like to share a breakfast picnic with me. Let's see what we have in here."

I unfurl the tablecloth, then set out a bowl of grapes and a plate with a single donut. "Gee," I say with an overtone of confusion, "there are plenty of grapes, but only one donut. And there are ... (I take a quick count of noses) ... ten of you! What are we going to do?"

"We can share the donut," the children suggest.

"That's a great idea!" I answer. I ask one of the children to pass out napkins; then we pass the food around, each child taking a few grapes and breaking off a piece of the donut. I am pleased to note that everyone is very careful to take only a small piece to

172

ensure there is enough for everyone. Consequently, more than half of the donut is left when it comes back to me. I take another piece and pass it around again.

"Why do we eat?" I ask next.

"Because donuts are GOOD!"

"Because things taste good."

"Because we're hungry."

The latter is the response I was hoping for. "Yes, we eat for all of those reasons. We eat because our bodies need food to create bone and muscle, and to give us energy. When we don't eat, we get hungry. That's our body's way of telling us it's time to eat.

"So," I continue, "have you been enjoying summer?" This brings affirmative nods but no vocal responses; I seem to have an unusually quiet mix of children this morning.

"How many of you have been separated from good friends this summer because you or they have gone away on vacation?" Numerous hands go up.

"Did you miss your friend a lot?" I ask one of the older kids.

"Yes," she answers; "I was glad to get back so we could play together again."

173

"It's tough to be separated from good friends. It sort of makes your heart hungry when you're apart, just as our bodies get hungry when we need to eat. I brought these grapes and this donut to try to help us understand something Jesus said. He was speaking to a big crowd of people and told them, 'I am the bread of heaven.' He wasn't talking about bread for physical hunger, but bread for this other kind of hunger, the hunger of the heart.

"All of us have eaten part of the same donut this morning, haven't we?" The children nod agreement.

"So, this single donut has become a part of all of us," I continue. "When Jesus said, 'I am the bread of heaven,' he also said, 'Whoever eats my flesh and drinks my blood will have eternal life.' But he wasn't talking about bread like this donut. He was talking about spiritual food, food for the heart.

"Just as we took the donut and grapes into our bodies this morning, Jesus was talking about taking him into ourselves, making his spirit a part of us. When we do that, we are connected to him and to God forever; when we make Jesus a part of who we are, we have a relationship that will never die. And through him, we are all connected to one another. We are the church, the body of Christ. And through us, Jesus reaches out to embrace the world with his love."

Through The Eyes Of Love

"But now in Christ Jesus you who once were far off have been brought near by the blood of Christ. For he is our peace ..."
— Ephesians 2:13-14a

Theme: *Love; differences; tolerance.*

Visual Aid: *A pair of binoculars.*

This morning I have brought a small pair of binoculars and begin by asking the children, "How many of you have ever used binoculars?"

Every child present raises a hand. Giving the binoculars to the nearest child, I suggest that she look through them and pass them on. While this process continues, I ask, "What happens when you look through binoculars?"

"It brings things that are far away closer," the children answer.

"That's right," I agree. "Looking through binoculars makes it possible for us to see things that are far away more clearly. It makes them seem closer. It changes the way in which we are able to see them."

"Well, the reason I brought binoculars this morning is because of something Saint Paul wrote in his letter to the Ephesians. Paul was writing to these folks about the differences which had always separated Jews and Gentiles. He said it was like the Jews were the ones who were close to God and the Gentiles had always been at a distance. But Jesus changed all that. Paul told the Ephesians that Jesus brought near even those who had been far away because the differences that had always separated them just didn't matter any more. They could be at peace with one another and all be part of a single church because they shared one thing: their belief in Jesus as the Christ.

"Have any of you ever disagreed with someone else?" The children think about this and most of them nod affirmatively as they recall their own experiences.

"I got mad at my brother once!" a little boy announces.

I thought to myself that this had probably occurred more than once, as I said, "But you still love him, don't you?"

"Well, yes," the boy replied. "He's my brother!"

"I think what you've just said, Tommy, is a good lesson for us all. It doesn't matter that you disagree with Alex, or even that you get angry with him sometimes; you still love him because he is your brother. Your love overcomes your differences and draws you near to one another again — sort of like the binoculars overcome the distance between you and objects that are far away.

"That's what Paul was saying to the Ephesians. He was telling the Jews that the love of Jesus was enough to overcome their differences with the Gentiles; that because of Jesus, they were all brothers and sisters in Christ — just as Tommy loves Alex no matter what, because he's Tommy's brother.

"Sometimes it is really difficult to overlook differences we have with another person. Sometimes other people's ideas can seem so strange to us that we even become angry with them for thinking what they think. Sometimes other people seem so different we react to them with fear and even hatred.

"Perhaps you have heard a conversation something like this: One person might say, 'I don't like Amos.' A second person might say, 'Why not?' And the first person might say, 'Because he talks funny.'

"The way Amos talks may make him different, but that is no reason to dislike or hate him. But the first person in that conversation chose not to like Amos rather than to try to understand him and overcome the difference that divided them.

"Jesus didn't let differences divide. Jesus broke down all those barriers, way back when Paul was writing to the Ephesians about the Jews and the Gentiles, and today too. Jesus tells us to take a look at what is really important. Jesus tells us we sometimes need to look at things in a different way in order to overcome our differences, sort of like what happens when we look through binoculars. Jesus breaks down all the barriers that divide us from one another and draws us near to one another with his love. When we see one another the way Jesus does, we cannot hate. When we see each other through Jesus' eyes, we recognize that we are all part of the family of God, a family in which there are no strangers and in which differences do not matter."

Don't Lose Your Marbles!

"God did not give us a spirit of cowardice, but rather a spirit of power and of love and of self-discipline." — 2 Timothy 1:7

Theme: *Self-control; freedom of choice; peer pressure.*

Visual Aid: *A muslin bag filled with marbles, part of which are corralled together in a net bag.*

As the children group themselves on the chancel steps, I hold up a muslin bag and shake it. The contents give off a telltale clicking sound. "Do you know what I have in this bag?" I ask.

"MARBLES!" the children reply with evident glee.

"That's right, and I'm going to need a little help here. Melissa, would you hold these?" I hand her part of the marbles which are secured in a net bag. Then I turn to Tommy and ask, "Would you hold these?"

He extends one hand to take the muslin bag. However, this is not what I have in mind. "You may want to use both hands, Tommy," I suggest. As he puts his hands together, I pour into them the contents of the bag — *loose* marbles.

"Now," I address all of the children, "why did I ask Tommy to use both hands?"

"So he wouldn't spill his marbles," Ted answers.

"That's right, Ted," I agree. "But Melissa didn't need two hands to hold the other marbles. How are Tommy's marbles different?"

"Tommy's are loose!" several children reply in chorus.

"That's right," I continue, "so he needed both hands to hang on to them."

"Have any of you ever heard the expression, 'You must have lost your marbles'?"

Several children nod affirmatively. I ask one of them, "What does it mean?"

"That you don't know where they are," he answers. Once again I am reminded how concretely and literally young children think. Jason, who is older, waves his hand wildly to get my attention. I nod to him and he says, "If you've lost your marbles it could mean you've gone crazy."

"Yes, it could mean you had some real marbles and actually lost them. But often when people say, 'You've lost your marbles,' it's an expression that means you've done something really crazy.

"I know some people think I'm crazy for bringing marbles to church. But I brought them today because I want to talk to you about 'self-control.' What does it mean to have 'self-control'?"

"**Not** to go crazy," Terry says matter-of-factly, emphasizing the word "not."

"Yes," I reply. "It has something to do with making a choice about how we behave. Sometimes it takes a lot of self-control to make the right choice, to do the right thing, particularly when our friends may be encouraging us or daring us to do something we know isn't right. For example, what would you do if someone hit you?" I ask.

"I'd tell someone," Timothy answers.

"That's a good thing to do, Tim. And a lot safer than hitting the person back. What did Jesus say to do if someone hit you on the cheek?"

"He said to turn the other cheek, too," John replies.

"That's right, John. And that seems sort of crazy, doesn't it? But it reminds us that we have a choice, and while it is easy to respond to anger with anger, to violence with violence, to hatred with hatred, Jesus asks us to keep our cool, to make a choice to do the right thing — to follow his example and respond to anger, hatred, and violence with love, understanding, and compassion. Sometimes the right choice is not an easy choice, and sometimes we need help to stay in control of ourselves. Who helps us do that?"

"Our parents," Mary answers.

"Jesus," Bobby says.

"The church?" Jennifer asks.

179

"Yes, our parents help us make right choices, as do Jesus and our church family," I affirm. "When we don't feel courageous or strong enough to make the right choice on our own, we can call on our family and friends for help and we can turn to Jesus and God in prayer. Well, I want to give you an opportunity to practice self-control right here in church this morning. I want every one of you to take a marble." At this suggestion, there is a noticeable intake of breath from some of the adults in the sanctuary.

"Now, this is VERY important ..." I stop speaking until I have made eye contact with every child present. Then I continue: "I want you to have enough self-control that you don't play with your marbles until AFTER church — and whatever you do, don't drop them during the rest of our worship service. If you think you might have trouble, you can ask your mom or dad to hold your marble for you until later.[1]

"Okay, let's have a prayer before you go. God, thank you for the gifts of the spirit, which include self-control. Thank you for giving us the wisdom, direction, and courage it takes to make the right choices. Help us always to remember that we CAN choose how we behave. We offer this prayer in Jesus' name. Amen."

---

1. Because the Youth Choir sang at our early service on this Sunday, the average age of the children was considerably older than at the second service. During early worship, five marbles were dropped and went bouncing across the sanctuary's hardwood floors, under the pews, to the back of the church. The younger children, during the second service, did not drop a single marble.

No Strings Attached

"For God so loved the world that he gave his only Son, so that everyone who believes in him may not perish but may have eternal life." — John 3:16

Theme: *Generosity; stinginess.*

Visual Aid: *A stuffed animal with a "leash" of rubber bands.*

"My stuffed cat, Cecil, and I would like to invite all the young people to come join us on the steps at this time." So do I begin yet another children's sermon, trying to add a little variety by including the stuffed toy in my invitation, the name of the cat coming to me simultaneously with the thought.

As the children settle down, I ask one of them to hold "Cecil," to whom I have attached a "leash" of rubber bands. As I hand the cat to Marie, I keep my fist closed around the end of the "leash." Before Marie has an opportunity to notice the rubber bands, I give them a tug. Surprised, she nearly drops the toy.

"What happened?" I ask, as she now clings more tightly to the stuffed cat.

"There's a string of rubber bands attached," Marie replies.

"A string of rubber bands? Oh, like a leash ... and when I handed you the cat, I didn't let go of the rubber bands, did I?"

"No," Marie answers, cringing as I continue to maintain tension on the "leash."

"So, I didn't give Cecil to you completely, did I?"

"No," Marie acknowledges.

"What would I have to do to make it easier for you to hold Cecil? What would I have to do to give him to you freely?"

"Let go of the rubber bands!" several children answer in chorus. Marie winces noticeably at their suggestion.

"That's right," I answer. "In order to give completely, I need to let go — very gently, so as to not pop Marie with the rubber bands." Marie grins and breathes a sigh of relief.

"Well," I continue, "the reason I brought Cecil this morning to help me with this little demonstration is that I wanted to talk with you today about 'generosity.' That's a big word. I wonder, do any of you know what it means?"

Tina, seated on the back row, politely raises her hand. I nod to her and she says, "Being nice and giving."

"Yes," I agree. " 'Generosity' means giving, being generous. Does it mean giving completely or hanging onto what you give?"

"Completely," the children assure me.

"So, if I give you something with strings — or in Cecil's case, rubber bands — attached, am I being generous?"

"No," the children answer.

"Well, I wonder, does anyone know what the opposite of 'being generous' is?" I should have seen their answer coming.

"Not being generous," comes the very practical, literal response.

It is difficult not to laugh as I continue. "Not being generous ... that's right. Another word for that is 'stingy.' Is that a word any of you know?" The children admit familiarity with this word, usually applied with regard to competition with siblings over prized personal possessions.

"So, when I asked Marie to hold Cecil but kept holding onto the 'leash,' I was being stingy. There are many ways to give something to another person, and some of those ways are not generous but stingy. If I give something out of the goodness of my heart, out of love for someone else, I am being generous. But I might also give out of a sense of duty, a feeling that it is something I have to do. In that case, I would be holding back, not giving completely. I would not be completely happy about what I was doing, and whatever I gave with that attitude would still be tied to me. My unhappiness would keep me from letting go of the gift.

"I might also give something to another person out of a sense of pride. For example, if I was walking along and found Tommy here had fallen into a ditch, I would help him out, and helping him would be a gift to him. If I did that just because I love Tommy as a fellow human being, that would be generosity. But if I did it only so others would see me help and think what a nice person I am, then I would be helping out of a sense of pride. I would be helping Tommy, not because he needed help, but because of what I would get out of doing it. That's a very stingy way to give too, not generous at all.

"Our example of how to be generous comes to us from God. God gave us his only son, Jesus, with no strings attached at all. God gave to us completely just because God loves us so much and wants to be with us. And Jesus showed us how to live generously, giving from the heart to any people who asked it of him, regardless of who they were or what society thought of them.

"Jesus gave himself away to people who were sick, poor, hungry, tired, dishonest — people from whom most folks back then turned away. Jesus didn't judge them; he only answered their cries for help, their needs for acceptance and love. He gave himself completely away with no thought of getting anything back. He gave himself to them and he gives himself to us, with no strings attached.

"That's what Cecil and I wanted to tell you about today, how to be generous like Jesus. When you give someone a gift, give it completely, from your heart. Just let go, out of love."

Catfishing?

"He got into one of the boats, the one belonging to Simon, and asked him to put out a little way from the shore. Then he sat down and taught the crowds from the boat. When he had finished speaking, he said to Simon, 'Put out into the deep water and let down your nets for a catch.' Simon answered, 'Master, we have worked all night long but have caught nothing. Yet if you say so, I will let down the nets.' When they had done this, they caught so many fish that their nets were beginning to break. So they signaled their partners in the other boat to come and help them. And they came and filled both boats, so that they began to sink. But when Simon Peter saw it, he fell down at Jesus' knees, saying, 'Go away from me, Lord, for I am a sinful man!' For he and all who were with him were amazed at the catch of fish that they had taken."

— Luke 5:3-9

Theme: Trust; problem solving.

Visual Aid: A pole about four feet long with a nylon rope attached to one end. The other end of the rope has a cat toy tied to it.

———————

"Would one of you hold this for me?" I extend a long plastic pole with a nylon line tied to one end. Something that looks rather like a rabbit's foot is tied to the end of the line. "What do you think this is?" I ask the fascinated children.

"A fishing pole!" comes their immediate response.

"Yes, a fishing pole. But it looks a little different than most fishing poles I've ever seen. What do you think I might fish for with this one?"

"A rabbit?" Obviously Maria has noticed the fake-fur item tied to the end of the line.

"Well, no, not a rabbit. But that's a close guess."

"Something blind?" That was certainly an intriguing idea. I wondered at the other thought processes going on in Henry's mind.

"No, not something blind. Whatever it is has to be able to see what's on the end of the line."

"A bear?"

"Wow! A bear? No, I don't think I'd want to try to go fishing for a bear. I might have more than I could handle.

"Actually, my cats received this 'fishing pole' as a present from our housekeeper. It's a cat toy. And it's a very unusual fishing pole, isn't it?"

Suddenly one of the older boys, whom I can always count on for humor, interrupts with his response to what one might fish for with this pole:

"CATFISH!"

"Well, that's a clever idea, Andrew," I answer, "a little different than fishing for cats. But, now that we've figured out what we might do with this pole, let's take a look at fishing in the Bible. Peter, James, and John were all fishermen, you know. However, when they went fishing they didn't use poles. Do any of you have any idea what they did use to catch fish?"

"Sticks?" (A reasonable response. "Handle it gently," I caution myself, "so as not to discourage this child who has dared to answer.")

"Well, I can see since we've been talking about poles that sticks would make sense, Jeremy, but the disciples used something else."

"Nets," comes the next suggestion.

"Yes, they used nets, great big ones. They used nets so they could catch lots of fish at once. And usually, that's what happened. But, there was a time that Peter, James, and John went out fishing and fished all night long — and they didn't catch ANYTHING! Gosh! That would really be a long night, wouldn't it? To fish ALL NIGHT and not catch ANYTHING?

"The next day Jesus was in one of the boats with the disciples. He saw that their boats were empty and said, 'Let your nets down here for a catch.'

"Peter answered him, saying, 'We fished all night, right in this spot, and didn't catch anything. But since you say to do it again, we will.' So, one more time they let their nets down, and guess what happened? They caught a LOT of fish!" ("Catfish!" Andrew interjects, eliciting laughter from us all. Then I continue.) "In fact, they caught so many fish that the nets started to break and tear apart. The fish were so heavy and there were so many of them that the boats began to sink! They had caught a LOT of fish! Now why did they catch so many?"

"Because Jesus told them to fish there?"

"Yes, but what made them do what Jesus said to do?"

"Their love for him?"

"Yes. And what else? They fished there because they..."

"Trusted him?"

"Yes, they fished there because they loved Jesus and trusted him. Sometimes there are things in our lives that we have problems with. Sometimes we think we have to depend just on ourselves to solve those problems. But that's not true. Who can we go to with our problems? Who is always there to help us out if we will only ask and trust?"

"Jesus!" several children respond.

"Catfish!" Andrew mutters.

"You're being silly," I tell him. "And, of course, I'm NEVER silly. You KNOW that!" Most of the children realize I am teasing and grin.

"So, when we have problems, and all of us do sometimes, it's important to remember that we don't have to handle them alone. We can take them to Jesus in prayer and ask for his help. He will help us solve them, just as he helped the disciples with their fishing."

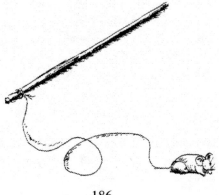

Earthen Vessels

"For it is the God who said, 'Let light shine out of darkness,' who has shone in our hearts to give the light of the knowledge of the glory of God in the face of Jesus Christ. But we have this treasure in clay jars, so that it may be made clear that this extraordinary power belongs to God and does not come from us."
— 2 Corinthians 4:6-7

Theme: *Love; self-esteem.*

Visual Aid: *Several small clay jars.*

"I've brought two small things this morning to pass around so you can look at them. What are they?"

"Vases!" some children answer.

"Little jars," others suggest.

"Well, what do you think they are made of?"

"Glass?" comes the first tentative response.

"That's a good guess. They are very much like glass vases and jars. But they are made of something else."

"Clay!" a more certain child pronounces with a hint of "Aha!" in his voice.

"Clay. That's right. Where do we get clay?" In asking this question I find myself hoping no one comes back with, "At the store."

"We get it out of the ground," comes the welcome answer.

"Yes, we get it out of the ground," I agree. "So, clay comes from the earth; it is a type of earth. We could say these little clay jars are made of earth.

"Now, in Genesis there is a story about God doing something with clay or earth taken from the ground. God took the clay and made something. Does anyone know what that was?"

"People!" Melinda pronounces, triumphantly.

"Yes. God took the clay (the earth), formed it into people, and breathed life into them.

"Well, that's interesting. These little jars are made of clay and so are people, including every one of you! Isn't that amazing?

"There is another scripture that might help us understand all of this a little better. In Second Corinthians it says, 'We have a treasure in earthen vessels...' When you hear the hear the word 'treasure,' what do you think of?"

"Gold!" comes the glittering response.

"Any particular kind of gold?" I ask.

"Gold coins!"

"Jewelry!"

"I often think about those kinds of treasures too," I respond, "and yet, when I read the scripture about having a treasure in earthen vessels, I wonder what that means. I look at these little earthen vases I have brought this morning and think, well, I might put a gold coin in one of them, but I don't think that's what the scripture is talking about. I think the scripture is talking about the earthen vessels that are people.

"Remember? God took that clay from the earth and made human beings. So, according to the scripture, there's some kind of treasure inside of each one of you. I think that treasure is the spirit of Jesus Christ. Just as I might put a gold coin inside this earthen jar, God has put Christ's spirit inside of every one of you as a very precious treasure.

"What does it mean to have Jesus' spirit inside of you?"

"It means we have love," says a little voice from the back of the group.

"Yes, we have love inside of us. And that love is there to be shared with other people. I hope this week you'll think about that very special treasure inside of you, the spirit of Jesus. I hope you'll have lots of opportunities this week to share that treasure, to love your families and friends. And whenever you see a little jar or vase made of clay, a little earthen vessel, I hope you'll remember the treasure you hold inside and know just how special you are to God. Why else would God put something so precious within you?"

Alone

" 'Go therefore and make disciples of all nations, baptizing them in the name of the Father and of the Son and of the Holy Spirit, and teaching them to obey everything that I have commanded you. And remember, I am with you always, to the end of the age.' " — Matthew 28:19-20

Theme: *Jesus' constant presence; faith; discipleship.*

Visual Aid: *A dictionary.*

———————

"I've brought a big book with me today. Does anyone know what it is?" Eager hands shoot up as the older children recognize the volume. I nod to one of them.

"It's a dictionary!" he announces.

"Yes, it's a dictionary," I respond. "What does one find in a dictionary?"

"Words!" many of the children reply in concert.

"Yes, WORDS!" I agree, with emphasis on "words." "I love words," I continue. "I was thinking about a particular word this week, the word 'alone.' Have any of you ever been alone?"

The hand of every child is raised, some more slowly than others, as they think back to times when they have been alone.

"I think most of us have been alone at some time or another," I continue.

"Well, the neat thing about a dictionary is that when you look up a word, sometimes it tells you other words which that word is made of. When I looked up 'alone,' I found out that it is made up of two words. Now, if someone had told me that, I would have thought, 'Okay. "A" is one word and "lone" is the other word.' But, that's not the way it is. 'Alone' is made up of 'all,' a - l - l, and 'one,' o - n - e. One of the l's was dropped when these two words were put together to make 'alone.'

190

"But if 'alone' is 'all' plus 'one ...' That seems kind of strange for a word that means to be by yourself, doesn't it? Because, if it's 'all' PLUS 'one,' you have added something. And if you add something, you are no longer alone." I can see by the looks on their young faces that the children are wondering where I am going with this idea.

"Well, I want you to remember, whenever you think you're alone, you aren't. You are 'all' plus 'one.' Do you know who that 'plus one' is?" Aaron, a youngster who is always willing to risk a response, raises his hand. I nod for him to speak.

"Jesus," he says with a big smile.

"Jesus! That's right. Now we just heard nine of your friends make their confession of faith that Jesus is their personal savior; that Jesus is with them, an important part of their lives — just as Jesus is with every one of you. Because you are never really alone; you're 'all' plus...." I pause for the children's response, which comes immediately:

"ONE!" they announce in chorus.

"That's right. And Jesus is the 'One,' " I reiterate one more time. "So, the next time you feel like you are alone, I hope you'll remember what we talked about today. Then you need never, ever feel totally alone again. You are 'all' plus 'One,' and that 'One' loves you very much."

Don't Run Away!

"Now the word of the LORD came to Jonah son of Amittai, saying, 'Go at once to Nineveh, that great city, and cry out against it; for their wickedness has come up before me.' But Jonah set out to flee to Tarshish from the presence of the LORD."

— Jonah 1:1-3a

Theme: *Avoidance; discipleship; God's will; problem solving.*

Visual Aid: *I did not use one. However, most children's Bibles contain a picture of Johah and the great fish.*

———————

"How many of you have ever been asked to do something you didn't want to do?" Hands immediately fly into the air as bright voices begin to tell me of those things that torment their young existence:

"Make my bed!"

"Take a bath!"

"Fold washcloths!"

"Put on my shoes when I'm in the house and I don't think I need them!"

Surprised at the absence of one particular answer, I tease the children with the comment, "I suppose you all enjoy cleaning your rooms?"

"OH NO!" comes the unanimous, vehement reply.

"No? Well, no one mentioned it. I just thought I'd better check. I didn't enjoy cleaning my room when I was your age either — in fact, I still don't. But sometimes it's necessary to do things we don't want to do. The Bible contains many stories of people who were asked to do things they didn't want to do. One of these people was Jonah. Who can tell me something about Jonah?"

"He was a man who went out in a boat," comes the initial response.

"Why?" I ask.

"Because God asked him to talk to some people and he didn't want to."

I am impressed by these children's knowledge of the story. "Yes, God asked him to talk to the people of Nineveh. So he decided to run away from God. That's why he was in the boat. But what happened?"

"He got swallowed by a whale!" several children exclaim together.

"Yes, there was a fierce storm, and Jonah ended up in the ocean where a big fish swallowed him up."

At this statement Tashia raises her hand to get my attention. I nod to her. She holds her hands outstretched as far as they will go and says, "It was at least this big!"

"Yes," I agree, "it was at least that big!" Then, looking around at the group of inquiring faces I ask, "Can you imagine being swallowed by a fish?"

As many little heads shake the answer, Tommy speaks. "No," he says, "I'll bet he didn't like it very much."

"Who," I ask innocently, "Jonah or the fish?"

"Well, Jonah, of course!" Tommy replies, somewhat impatiently. But it is evident that some young minds have been stretched with the thought that the fish might have had feelings too.

"So, what happened to Jonah after he had been in the belly of the fish for three days?"

"The fish spit him out!" several children answer in unison.

"That's right. The fish spit him out, not into the water, but onto dry land. While Jonah was in the fish, he had lots of time to think about God and what had happened when he had tried to run away from the task God wanted him to do. When he finally got out of the fish, Jonah knew there was no place on earth where he could run completely away from God.

"Jonah also knew, because God had come after him and saved him, that God loved him even though he had disobeyed. So Jonah went to Nineveh and did what God had asked him to do in the first place.

"Sometimes our parents or teachers or friends ask us to do things we really don't want to do. We can refuse, disobey, even run away. But eventually, like Jonah, we have to come back and the task is still waiting. Running away is not often the best way to solve a problem. So, the next time you're asked to help out by folding clothes, or making your bed, or even cleaning your whole room, maybe you'll find the task easier if you remember the story of Jonah. God loved Jonah and needed Jonah's help, just as the people asking you to do these things you don't like to do need your help. I'll bet they love you too."

God Was A Child Too

"Now every year his parents went to Jerusalem for the festival of the Passover. And when he was twelve years old, they went up as usual for the festival. When the festival was ended and they started to return, the boy Jesus stayed behind in Jerusalem, but his parents did not know it. Assuming that he was in the group of travelers, they went a day's journey. Then they started to look for him among their relatives and friends. When they did not find him, they returned to Jerusalem to search for him. After three days they found him in the temple, sitting among the teachers, listening to them and asking them questions. And all who heard him were amazed at his understanding and his answers."

— Luke 2:41-47

Theme: *School; understanding; confession; compassion; revelation; unconditional love.*

Visual Aid: *A picture of myself when I was four years old and my first grade report card.*

About twenty children have come forward at my invitation to sit on the chancel steps. I begin by asking, "Is anyone here this morning four years old?"

Brenda hesitatingly raises her hand. I acknowledge her response with a smile and direct my next comment to her.

"I've got a surprise for you: I was four once! And I can prove it! I've brought a picture this morning which I'll ask Brenda to pass around so you can all take a closer look at it. It's a picture of me when I was four years old."

As I pass the picture to Brenda, I recall how difficult it was for me as a child to imagine that adults had ever been children too; pictures always helped.

"After that picture was taken," I continue, "I naturally kept getting older. After a couple of years, guess what happened?"

This question is greeted with puzzled expressions, so I answer. "I went to school! How many of you are in school?" With this query, about half of the children raise their hands.

"Well, one of the things that happens in school is that every so often you get a grade card, don't you?" Several children nod their affirmation; some of them roll their eyes as an expression of their distaste for grade reports.

"I was thinking about that this morning because I know grades are coming up soon for those of you who are in school. So, I brought something else to show you this morning: a very, very old grade card — mine, from the first grade. Let's see ... The date on the front is February 2, 1953. Wow! I must have gone to school with the dinosaurs!"

Many of the children laugh at this and shake their heads in disagreement. "You don't think I'm quite that old?" I ask them. Their heads shake "no" again. "Well, thank you."

I proceed to open up the report card and show them the inside where all the grades are recorded. They notice the teacher has written an extensive commentary as well.

"I'm just going to read one paragraph of this to you," I tell them.

"Kathy has shown much improvement. She works well with our group. She's trying hard to develop good listening habits. Sometimes Kathy needs my help in seeing that she is an attentive listener when someone else is talking."

I stop reading and ask the children, "Do any of you ever have that problem?" My question elicits their grins; after all, who hasn't been caught talking in class at one time or another?

"Well, the point of this discussion," I continue, "is that, believe it or not, your parents were children once. Now, because your parents used to be children, they used to be in school, and they had problems from time to time just like you do. That's why most of the time when you have some sort of trouble they are able to understand — because they remember how it was for them.

196

"Well, for you, whether you are struggling with homework or even if you have gotten in trouble for doing something you really shouldn't have (like not listening when someone else is talking), it's important for you to be able to talk with your parents about it and know that they will probably understand how you feel. They'll even understand if you have difficulty telling them about your problem, because they remember how hard it was sometimes for them to tell their parents about things.

"There's someone else who understands too — God. God came down to earth in Jesus Christ. Jesus was born, had parents, and was a little child at one time, just like all of you. So God knows how we feel when we're in trouble or when we're struggling with something that seems too difficult.

"God always understands, and most of the time, your parents will understand your struggles and your troubles too. And no matter what, God and your parents always love you."

Snow Forts

"Put away from you all bitterness and wrath and anger and wrangling and slander, together with all malice, and be kind to one another, tenderhearted, forgiving one another, as God in Christ has forgiven you." — Ephesians 4:31-32

Theme: *Anger; reconciliation; forgiveness; unconditional love.*

Visual Aid: *None. This message employs the children's awareness of a recent snowfall to capture their interest.*

————————

"Something exciting happened earlier this week. On Monday, it was fairly warm for this time of year. Then Wednesday it got cold, and by Thursday ... What happened with the weather on Thursday?"

"It snowed!" come the excited replies.

"Yes, it snowed. It was the first snow since last winter, wasn't it?" The children nod their agreement.

"Do all of you like to play in snow?" The sanctuary erupts with a cacophony of children's voices assuring me that of course they like to play in snow! Snow is FUN!

"Okay!" I interrupt. "I'm convinced! Now, I have another question for you. Who here has ever made a snow fort?" Several hands, all belonging to boys, shoot up. I find myself wondering if I'm the only girl who ever did that sort of thing.

"Making a snow fort is a lot of work, isn't it?" I continue. The children who are experienced in the fine art of snow fort-making agree.

"Well, then, why do you go to all that trouble?" I ask.

"So we can play in them ..."

"... and have snowball fights!"

"You're telling me that you do all that work so you can FIGHT with each other?" I ask with mock incredulity.

"No, we're not REALLY fighting; we're playing."

"Oh, I see. You go to all that trouble to PLAY like you're fighting ..." Grins begin to appear on the children's faces as they recognize that I am toying with them.

"Well, if you've taken all the time and effort required to build a snow fort to play in, I assume it lasts a LONG time — maybe even all winter?"

"No!" the children protest. "The walls melt when the sun comes out."

"Oh, I see. So if the sun were to come out the very next day, the fort would begin to melt and all your hard work would disappear."

"Yes," they agree.

"I'm asking all of these questions because I saw some children building a snow fort Thursday evening. The walls of rolled-up snow caused me to think about other kinds of walls in our lives. Do any of you ever get angry?"

Andrew puts on a face of wide-eyed innocence and, trying not to crack a smile, says, "Oh NO! Not EVER!"

I respond with my "I-don't-think so!" look and his facade of innocence breaks into the grin he was trying to contain.

"Yes, I get angry sometimes," he acknowledges.

"So do I!" several more voices chime in.

"Of course you do," I answer. "All of us get angry once in a while. Even Jesus got angry sometimes. But when we get angry with one another, that anger is like a wall between us. Now, think back to the snow forts we were just talking about. What melted those walls?"

"The sun!" come twenty voices in unison.

"Yes, the sun's heat melted the snow walls. But what about walls of anger? What does it take to melt them?"

This is a tough question for youngsters, so they do not respond immediately. Finally, one of them says, "You make up with each other."

"That's a good answer," I reply. "If you make up, you are no longer angry with each other, right?" The children nod affirmatively.

199

"Would it be fair to say you have forgiven each other for whatever it was that made you angry in the first place?" The nods of agreement come again.

"So, what we're really saying is that forgiveness melts walls of anger just as the sun melts walls of snow. You know, being able to forgive people is one way to show that you recognize their worth in God's eyes. That's why Jesus taught us to forgive each other, just as God forgives us when we do things we shouldn't.

"God can do that because, no matter what we do, God still loves us. It's important that we extend this same grace to the people who are part of our lives. Even though we get angry with them sometimes, we need to understand that they are God's children and we need to do our best to love them.

"One way to show others we love them is to forgive them when they do something that makes us angry. It is important to melt those walls of anger before more anger gets piled on top and the walls become so huge it seems like nothing will ever break them down."

Costumed Christians

"Above all, clothe yourselves with love, which binds everything together in perfect harmony." — Colossians 3:14

Theme: *Discipleship; love; tolerance; Halloween.*

Visual Aid: *None. The children's excitement about Halloween piques their interest.*

"This is October, right?" The assembled children nod affirmatively.

"And October has 31 days?" A few knowing grins break out as young minds realize where I must be headed.

Receiving a positive response, I then ask, "Does October thirty-first have any special significance for any of you?"

"Yes!" come the now-vocalized replies. "It's Halloween!"

I look slightly puzzled and ask, "Halloween? What does that mean?"

"It means you go to people's houses and ask for candy," Bethany says.

"You go trick-or-treating!" several other children offer.

"Trick-or-treating? Asking for candy? Why would I do that?" I ask, continuing to pretend I do not understand.

"Because it's fun!" several children say with obvious anticipation of their upcoming foray.

"Well," I go on, "what's fun about it?"

"You get to dress up in a costume!" Sally announces.

"A costume?" I question. "Now that does sound like fun. Are any of you planning to go trick-or-treating in a costume on Halloween?"

Little heads nod with eager affirmation. I begin to ask what costumes they have chosen.

"A dancer!"

201

"An alligator!"

"A butterfly!"

These answers come along with acknowledgments from other children that they have not yet decided what to "be." I had expected answers like "Ninja Turtle!" and all sorts of monsters. I find it refreshing to have such delightful choices as these children have made. Perhaps it is only older children who gravitate toward the heroes and the hideous.

I continue with a reminiscence from my own childhood, of the costume I wore the October I was five. "My parents turned me into a black cat for Halloween that year. The costume had a great long tail, stuffed with rags. It seemed very long and got very heavy to carry before the night was over. But I couldn't just drag it. I knew cats walked with their tails up. Besides, if I dragged it, the material would get a hole in it and the rags would come out!

"As I was thinking about Halloween this morning, and wondering what costumes you might have decided to wear, I found myself considering how a person might dress as a Christian. Do you have any ideas?"

Immediately the children's faces twist into thoughtful concentration. Finally Brian says, "A priest!"

"That would work," I acknowledge. "What else?"

Much to my delighted surprise, Linda suggests, "You could dress as yourself."

"Yes!" I agree. "Because being a Christian doesn't depend on whether you're dressed up in a suit or wearing rags, does it? Being a Christian means following the example of Jesus and being just who God created you to be — yourself!

"Still," I wonder out loud, "how would I know you are a Christian if you were just being yourself? If it didn't depend on how you looked or how you were dressed, what would tell me?"

As the children's puzzled silence grows, I continue. "Let me give you a hint. There's a song that ends with the words, 'And they'll know we are Christians by our love.' "

Eyes light up with understanding. "They'll know by how we act! They'll know by how we treat each other." (Children are so wise.)

202

"Yes, they'll know by our actions, by our love. Being yourself means living from your heart. I hope you all have fun on Halloween. And, as you turn into alligators, dancers, butterflies, and whatever else you decide upon, remember to be kind to the other costumed creatures you meet. Remember, beneath those costumes, who YOU are — Christian children full of love."

Ragman

"I give you a new commandment, that you love one another. Just as I have loved you, you should also love one another."
— John 13:34

Theme: *Unconditional love.*

Visual Aid: *A piece of cloth and a quilt block. (An entire pieced quilt would also suffice.)*

"Have you ever heard the word 'remnant'? No? Well, I'd like to talk about remnants this morning. A remnant is a leftover, a scrap. A good place to find remnants is at the fabric store. Often a small piece of material, usually a yard or less, is left on the end of a bolt of cloth after the rest of the bolt has been sold. This leftover piece is called a remnant.

"Remnants are not usually big enough to be as useful as larger pieces might be, so they are often sold at a reduced price. People who need just small pieces of material for handicrafts often buy remnants. Can all of you say 'remnant'?"

"There's another word that means close to the same thing which I'm sure all of you know: 'rag.' Where do we get rags?"

"You buy them!" Having just talked about going to the remnant table at the fabric store, I should have seen this coming.

"Well, yes," I continue. "Rags can be bought. But where else might we get rags? What happens when you get a hole in your sock? Do you fix it?"

"No! It gets thrown away!"

"But if you didn't throw it away, you'd have a rag, wouldn't you? If we tear a skirt or a pair of pants, or if we get a hole in the elbow of a jacket or sweater, we might patch it. But eventually, even the patch will wear out and you will have a piece of clothing which has become a rag. What do we do with rags?"

"Use them to clean!"

"Use them to wash dishes."

"Use them to wipe your hands on when you're working on the car."

"Use them for patches."

"Well, I can see by your answers that you are all familiar with rags. A long time ago there was an occupation that we don't hear much about any more: the ragman. The ragman would go door-to-door to collect, buy, and sell rags. Pieces of worn-out material, of no use to those who gave or sold them to him, were valued by the ragman because they provided his income.

"I was going through some rags in my attic the other day, and noticed how pretty some of them were. So, I cut them into strips and sewed the strips together to make this quilt square.

"Rags and remnants are very valuable to quilters who make beautiful covers from discarded, seemingly useless bits of material. As I was piecing this square together, I realized there was another 'ragman' whom we all know — only the rags he collected weren't material; they were people!

"You know, we are often afraid of people who are different from us. If people dress in a way that seems strange to us, we might avoid them, especially if their clothes are rags. But it may be that rags are all they can afford to wear.

"If someone has a disease we are afraid of, like AIDS, we might avoid that person too. Sometimes we avoid people with handicaps because we don't know how to act with them; we notice their handicaps and forget that they are people who have feelings, just like the rest of us.

"But there was a 'ragman' who taught us to love one another, unconditionally. He never turned away from the ragged people whom society pushed aside. He welcomed the blind, the broken, the torn, the dirty. The people whom others cast out in fear, he welcomed in love. He healed the brokenhearted, restored sight to the blind, cured lepers, and brought new wholeness to humanity. Do you know this ragman's name?

"Jesus!!"

"That's right. Jesus was the ragman. So the next time you get a hole in your sock, or tear a sleeve, or use a rag, remember a very special ragman whose love extends across the centuries to every one of us — right here, right now, every day of our lives. We know his love every time we open our hearts to one another."

God And Groundhogs

"O Most High, when I am afraid, I put my trust in you ... You have kept count of my tossings; put my tears in your bottle. Are they not in your record? ... In God, whose word I praise, in the LORD, whose word I praise, in God I trust; I am not afraid ... For you have delivered my soul from death, and my feet from falling, so that I may walk before God in the light of life."
— Psalm 56:2b-3, 8, 10-11a, 13

Theme: *Overcoming fear.*

Visual Aid: *A yardstick and a picture of a groundhog.*

"I'm sure you've noticed that I've brought a yardstick with me today." The children's heads nod affirmatively as their eyes watch the yardstick to see what I intend to do with it.

"I brought this to give you some idea of how long twenty inches is. From that end of the yardstick to where I have my thumb is twenty inches." The children look a bit puzzled, trying to figure out where I am going with this.

"Now, I'll move my thumb down this way a bit to show you how long 27 inches is." Again, the children watch closely. Finally, I ask the question they have been waiting for.

"What do you suppose I want to talk about today that is between twenty and 27 inches long?"

Andrew, seated on the back row, begins to wave his hand in the air. I nod to him and he answers, "A groundhog!"

"That's very good!" Already knowing what he would answer, I then ask, "How did you know that?"

"I know because I was here at the first service when you did this."

Gentle laughter from the congregation greets his reply.

"Well, now that you all have some idea of the size groundhogs grow to be, I have a picture of one for you to pass around so everyone can see what a groundhog looks like."

As the children pass the picture, I continue. "Groundhogs are burrowing animals. That means they dig holes in the ground to make their nests. During the winter, they hibernate in these nests. Who knows what 'hibernate' means?"

A number of hands go up and I hear the word "sleep" several times.

"Yes, it means to sleep for a long time. The groundhog hibernates — or sleeps — all winter. Does that sound like something you'd like to do?"

Some of the children grin as they think about my question. Others very seriously assure me they really would like to sleep all winter!

"We're talking about groundhogs today because this is Groundhog Day, the day on which it is traditional to watch the 'official' groundhog in Pennsylvania to determine whether or not it will see its shadow when it comes out of its burrow. Who knows what happens if the groundhog sees its shadow?"

Several hands go up. I nod to Sylvia. "We'll have six more weeks of winter," she says confidently.

"That's right," I continue. "According to tradition, if the groundhog sees its shadow, it will be afraid and return to its burrow — and we will have six more weeks of winter."

Andrew, the boy who was present during the earlier service and who has had some time to think about this, raises his hand. He obviously wants to say something, but I am not ready for what I think he might offer, so I ask, "What if the day is cloudy and the groundhog doesn't see its shadow?"

"Then it will be spring right now," two children respond together.

"That's right," I agree.

By now, Andrew has begun to look positively distressed, so I nod to him to speak.

"That doesn't make much sense," he observes. "What does the groundhog have to do with the weather?"

208

This is exactly the question I had anticipated from him. Now I find myself wondering how to explain the nature of folklore fairly quickly without losing the younger children's attention and trains of thought.

"Legends do not always make sense," I begin, "and this story is basically a legend. Sometimes people notice things that happen with the weather and look for ways to help them remember what to expect. Someone, somewhere, apparently noticed that if the weather was cloudy on February second, usually spring would come sooner than it would if the weather were sunny on that date. One way to remember this would be to create a story about the groundhog and its shadow.

"The groundhog really doesn't predict the weather. In fact, even the clouds or their absence do not predict the weather. But, more often than not, it seems that if we have cloudy weather on February second, winter will end much sooner than if the weather is sunny on that date." Andrew nods, thinking these ideas over — and causing me to wonder what he will bring up next week!

"Anyway, according to legend or tradition, if the groundhog sees its shadow, it will go back into its burrow. Why?"

"Because he's afraid of his shadow!" come numerous replies.

"So," I ask the children, "how many of you have ever been afraid of anything?" Hands begin to go up, and as some of the shyer children see others admitting they are afraid sometimes, their hands go up too. To the surprise of some, I raise my hand as well.

"Yes," I continue, looking around the group, "all of us are afraid sometimes. In fact, not only am I raising my hand with you, but all the people out there in the congregation in front of you could be raising their hands too, because *all* of us are afraid sometimes. And that's okay.

"But it's important to remember when you're afraid that you always have a place to run to. You always have a burrow to go to, just like the groundhog. And there's someone there to comfort you. Do you know who that might be?"

"A groundhog?" comes the logical guess.

"No, not really," I respond, "because I don't mean you would really go hide in a hole in the ground. Think of where you would go to feel safe if you were afraid."

Understanding dawns, brightening Maria's face as she says, "To my parents!"

"Yes," I agree. "And there is someone else you can turn to as well, someone who also loves you very much."

As Maria considers my statement, Andrew raises his hand. "All right, Andrew. Tell us whom else we might turn to when we are afraid."

"God!" he announces triumphantly.

"Yes, we can go to God when we are afraid. In fact, we can tell God anything at all and God will understand. So, the next time you are afraid, I hope you'll remember you always have some-place to go with that fear, whether it's to your parents, grandpar-ents, a friend, or God — who will be your friend too if you will let him.

"Sometimes when we are afraid, we feel like we just want to run away from everything and everyone. Then it's especially im-portant to remember that God is our friend. We can tell God all about what is bothering us. God always understands and never, ever leaves us to face our fears by ourselves, if we only have the courage to say, 'God, I need your help.' "

Epiphany

"Arise, shine; for your light has come, and the glory of the LORD has risen upon you. For darkness shall cover the earth, and thick darkness the peoples; but the LORD will arise upon you, and his glory will appear over you." — Isaiah 60:1-2

Theme: *Revelation; light; brokenness; life.*

Visual Aid: *An acorn which has begun to sprout and a plain-looking rock which has been split in two to reveal a bright red interior. (A geode would also be very useful for this sermon.)*

"I have a word I would like to ask you to think about this morning. It may be a new word for many of you. It's 'Epiphany.' Can you all say 'Epiphany'?"

Dutifully the children respond in chorus, "Epiphany!"

"That's very good. Now, does anyone know what it means?"

The children look thoughtful. Then two boys' hands shoot up almost simultaneously. I nod to the first, who says, "I think it has something to do with love." And so it does.

"That's true, Tommy," I answer. I nod then to the second boy whose hand is still aloft.

"I think it's before Easter," Alex responds.

Realizing he must have Epiphany confused with Lent, but not wanting to tell him his answer isn't right, I quickly review his words in my head and reply, "Yes, Epiphany is before Easter. In fact, it's way before Easter. It's just twelve days after Christmas!" Alex grins as if to acknowledge that I appreciate his risking a "wrong" answer in front of the entire congregation.

"Epiphany is also called 'Twelfth Night,' " I continue, "coming, as it does, twelve days after Christmas. It is set apart on the church calendar as the day the wise men traditionally arrived at the stable in Bethlehem and found Jesus, the Messiah, the Light of the

World. And because Jesus is thought of as the Light coming into human darkness, light is a symbol of Epiphany.

"We all need light in our lives, don't we?"

Most of the children nod in agreement, but some look doubtful. So I add, "Just think about it for a moment. Think how grumpy many of us get when we have cloudy weather day after day after day. We get grumpy because we aren't getting enough light! Do any of you ever get grumpy?"

"Oh no!" David assures me with a big grin. Most of the others laugh as Jonathan announces: "Well, I get grumpy sometimes."

"Ah! An honest man! How wonderful!" I respond.

"Well," I continue, "all living things need light to survive. I was out walking in the woods yesterday and came across this acorn. Now I know most of you have seen acorns, but we usually don't see them after they have started to sprout. As you can see, the plant inside of this acorn, which would become a big oak tree some day if it were left in the ground to grow, has split the shell. It had to split the shell in order to get to the sunlight. It needs the light to grow.

"On another walk a couple of months ago, I found this rock." I hold up an nondescript-looking rock.

"It's not very pretty, is it? In fact, it's an ugly rock. So you may wonder why I picked it up at all. But you see, it was split into two pieces when I found it." I separate the pieces and hand them to the children to pass around as I continue.

"As you can see, the rock is quite pretty on the inside; it's bright red. Now I never would have bothered to pick it up, I never would have seen its beauty, if it hadn't been split open — to the light.

"That makes me think about the things in life that split us apart sometimes. Sometimes we get hurt or something we like a lot breaks and we feel hurt. But I wonder if it's not those events in our lives, the ones that split us open, that cause us to grow like the seed, or cause us to reveal our inner beauty like the rock, or cause us to turn toward the Light of Jesus in our pain and hurt.

"We need light in our lives, and as Christians, we need Jesus, the Light of the World, in our lives in order to be truly alive. As

Tommy said, Epiphany has to do with love — the love of God, who sent his son into the world to bring us light. That's what Epiphany is all about.

"One more time now, so you don't forget, let's say the word we've been talking about together: 'Epiphany!' Yes, Epiphany. May its Light shine brightly in your lives this week."

Snow Angels

"In that region there were shepherds living in the fields, keeping watch over their flock by night. Then an angel of the Lord stood before them, and the glory of the Lord shone around them, and they were terrified. But the angel said to them, 'Do not be afraid; for see — I am bringing you good news of great joy for all the people: to you is born this day in the city of David a Savior, who is the Messiah, the Lord."   — Luke 2:8-11

Theme: *Advent; revelation; discipleship.*

Visual Aid: *A wooden manger with straw in it.*

"There's something on the steps this morning, taking up a LOT of room. What is it?" I ask.

"A manger!" respond those children who recognize it from Christmases past.

"Why is it on the chancel steps?" I continue.

"To celebrate Advent?" Sally questions.

"Yes," I reply, "to celebrate Advent, a time of waiting for someone to come. For whom are we waiting?"

"Jesus!" the children answer, with eagerness that gives a special energy and urgency to their voices.

"Yes, we're waiting for Jesus. This is December, it's Advent, and we're waiting for Jesus. But it doesn't *feel* like December, does it?" The children shake their heads negatively.

"It's gotten so warm the last two days it feels like spring," I suggest. "Yet, just last Monday, didn't we have snow and ice?" All the children nod to indicate "Yes."

"And, on Tuesday it was so cold it was hard to go outside even with a coat on. Now, today, some of us have come to church in short sleeves. In fact, some of you," I continue as I smile at Mary who is wearing a sleeveless dress, "have come with NO sleeves!

"Even so, the snow earlier this week caused me to remember times I had enjoyed playing in the snow when I was your age. What is your favorite thing to do in the snow?" I throw the question out for general responses, which come thick and fast.

"Sled!" several children announce with obvious glee.

"Make a snowman!" two more offer.

"Play in it!"

"Make snowballs!"

"Have snow fights!"

"Build snow forts!"

Their answers keep flying. These children are *involved* and obviously enjoy snow.

"Have any of you ever made a snow angel?" I ask.

"Oh, yes!" come many positive assurances.

"That used to be one of my favorite things to do in the snow," I continue. "Of course, I lived in Nebraska when I was your age, and the part we lived in was very flat. So, even though I had a sled, the only way I could use it was with another person. One of us had to pull the sled while the other one rode. That was a lot of work for the one doing the pulling, so we never did it for very long.

" 'Angel' comes from the Greek word *angelos*, which means 'messenger,' " I tell them. "Sometimes God sent angels as messengers to tell human beings things God wanted people to know.

Many of you remember the story of the shepherds who were in their fields watching their sheep. It was night, which meant it was dark. But suddenly there was a very bright light and an angel told them not to be afraid, that he had only come to tell them God's good news: that that very day, in the city of David, the Messiah had been born. Wow! That must have been quite an exciting experience! Imagine being visited by an angel — especially one with such good news!" The children's faces brighten as their imaginations go to work.

"You know," I continue, "there's something of an angel inside each one of you. Just like the angel that visited the shepherds that night, you can be God's messengers every time you tell someone about Jesus. Maybe the next time you make a snow angel, you'll remember that angels are God's messengers and think about what message of good news and great joy you might bring to the world."

The Wish

"Now faith is the assurance of things hoped for, the conviction of things not seen."   — Hebrews 11:1

Theme: *Hope; prayer; faith.*

Visual Aid: *A mechanical rabbit.*

"What is this?" I ask the assembled children as I hold up a small mechanical rabbit.

"A bunny!" several of the kids reply.

"Well now, since I brought a bunny rabbit today ..." I pause as if I'm uncertain of something "... is this Easter?"

"NO!" the children emphatically assure me.

"Well, if today isn't Easter, why did I bring a rabbit? I wonder ... Maybe you can help me figure this out. Is today any sort of holiday?"

"Yes," the children reply, "it's Father's Day."

"Oh, that's right. Now I remember. That's why I brought the rabbit." This elicits looks ranging from surprise to consternation. "I guess I'd better explain," I continue.

"When I was in the second grade, my father, who was in the army, got sent to a place called Korea. He was gone for a whole year and I missed him very much.

"But that still doesn't explain why I brought this rabbit. Let's see ... I'd better start the story sooner. Our family had gotten a kitten right before my dad had to leave for Korea. During the year he was gone, the kitten grew into a cat. She was a very nice cat too. But, for some reason, I had my heart set on having a white rabbit.

"However, the house we lived in wasn't ours. We rented it from the people who owned it. They had reluctantly agreed to let us have a cat, but a rabbit was out of the question because they thought it might mess up the house, and there was no place inside or outside to put a rabbit cage.

"Now, before I go any farther with this story, I need to know if any of you have ever heard of 'Brownies.' " Several children raise their hands. I nod to Jennifer, who says, "Brownies are really good! They're sort of chocolate cakes."

"Yes, that is one kind of brownie — and I agree, they are delicious! But the 'Brownies' I was thinking of are people!" Some of the children look surprised; others grin with understanding.

"You see, 'Brownies' was what the youngest age group of Girl Scouts was called when I was a child. The same year my dad went to Korea, I became a Brownie.

"The Brownies met once a week after school. At the end of every meeting, we would have what we called a wish circle. Can you guess what I wished for every week?"

"A white rabbit!" several children answer at once.

"That's right. And my mother, who was the leader of our Brownie troop, heard me make that wish, week after week.

"Then one day in the mail I received a package — from my dad! All the way from Korea! I was so excited I could hardly tear it open fast enough. And guess what I found inside?"

"A white rabbit?!"

"Yes! It wasn't a real one, of course. It was a mechanical toy, like this one. It was white and furry, and if I wound it up, it would hop — just like this." To the children's delight, I proceed to demonstrate with the rabbit I've brought.

"You see, my parents knew how badly I wanted a rabbit. They also knew I couldn't have a real, live one. The closest my mom and dad could come to fulfilling a wish that was obviously very important to me was to have my dad send me a toy white rabbit. And since I never thought I'd actually have ANY sort of rabbit — ever — receiving the wind-up bunny was like a miracle to me.

"Many years later, I was talking with a friend of mine who just happened to be a minister. We were talking about prayer and he suggested to me that prayer takes many forms. He said that God hears all of our desires, even the ones we don't usually think of as prayer, such as wishes, hopes, and dreams.

218

"As he spoke, I suddenly remembered the year my dad was in Korea. I remembered how I had wished for a white rabbit every week — and the tremendous love I felt when I opened the package from my dad and found the little toy rabbit.

"Because of my childhood experience, I understood what my minister friend was saying. When my father learned of my deep desire (I think my mother wrote him a letter), he did everything he could to fulfill my wishes. And that's how God is with our prayers, including our hopes, dreams, and wishes. Any expression we make of our very deepest desires, God hears.

"And, because of God's tremendous love for us, God will do everything God can to help us make those deepest desires become reality. Sometimes we need to take an active part and not just leave everything up to God, though.

"For example, if I had a deep desire to play the piano, I'd have to work hard at it — I'd have to do my part. But God would help me have the patience to practice.

"Other times, there may be nothing we can do to help the dream come true other than to keep alive the hope that it will. And that is the gift of faith, something the Bible calls 'the substance of things hoped for, the conviction of things not seen' (Hebrews 11:1).

"Sometimes the hopes and dreams and wishes we have may seem impossible. And without God's help, they might be. But faith is that gift of grace which keeps hopes and dreams alive as we place our trust and confidence in God. For, with God, nothing is impossible."

Idols

"Not to us, O LORD, not to us,
but to your name give glory,
for the sake of your steadfast love
and your faithfulness.
Why should the nations say,
'Where is their God?'
Our God is in the heavens;
he does whatever he pleases.
Their idols are silver and gold,
the work of human hands.
They have mouths, but do not speak;
eyes, but do not see.
They have ears, but do not hear;
noses, but do not smell.
They have hands, but do not feel;
feet, but do not walk;
they make no sound in their throats.
Those who make them are like them;
so are all who trust in them.

O Israel, trust in the LORD!
He is their help and their shield.
O house of Aaron, trust in the LORD!
He is their help and their shield.
You who fear the LORD, trust in the LORD!
He is their help and their shield."
— Psalm 115:1-11

Theme: *Idolatry; faith; trust.*

Visual Aid: *A wooden cow in a cardboard box.*

"We're going to talk about the second of the ten command-ments today. Does anyone know which one that is?" As the si-lence following my question grows, I coach the children.

"We talked about the first one last week, remember? It is 'You shall have no other gods.' Now, can you remember the second one?"

"Don't make graven images," Charles offers.

"That's right," I affirm. " 'Don't make graven images.' An-other way to say that is 'don't make idols.' God gave that com-mandment because God wants us to worship and trust only God, not something we have made ourselves.

"But sometimes, particularly sometimes when we are lost or afraid, it's hard to remember that. A long time ago, the Israelites had the same problem. They had escaped from Egypt and fol-lowed Moses and his brother Aaron into the wilderness.

"At a place called Mount Sinai, Moses left the people to go climb the mountain and talk to God. But he was gone such a very long time, the Israelites began to fear that Moses wasn't coming back. Furthermore, they had never actually seen God and they were beginning to think God wasn't real or that God had aban-doned them.

"Finally, they got so afraid, they went to Moses' brother, Aaron. They said, 'We're afraid out here in the wilderness without Moses and God. We want you to make us some gods to worship.'

"Now Aaron knew as well as any of them that God had ex-pressly forbidden the creation or worship of idols. But Aaron wanted to please the people. So, he decided to do what they asked, even though he knew it wasn't right.

"Aaron told the people to gather up all of their jewelry and bring it to him. When they had done so, Aaron put it all in a big pot and melted it. Then he poured the liquid gold into a mold and made a statue of a calf.

"The people were very pleased and had a huge celebration. They thanked Aaron and worshiped the golden calf, saying it was the god who had brought them out of Egypt!

"Needless to say, this made God very angry. After everything God had done for them to get them out of Egypt, they were worshiping and praising this statue, this idol, this golden calf Aaron had made for them!

At this point I open the cardboard box that has been in front of the children all this time, and lift out a wooden cow.

"This cow is not made out of gold; it's not even metal. But it should help us figure a few things out," I suggest.

"Let's take a close look at it. It has eyes, doesn't it?" The children nod affirmatively.

"Can it see?"

"No!" they respond.

"It's just a piece of wood!" Tommy adds.

"That's right," I agree. "Okay ... I see it has a nose. Can it smell?"

"No," the children answer as one voice.

"Well, it has legs ... Can it walk?"

"Of course not!" Jennifer says with an edge of impatience.

"The legs don't even move," Robert protests.

"Yes, you're right. Let's see ... It has a mouth. Can it speak?"

By this time most of the children are enjoying these obviously absurd questions because there is little doubt of the correct response, which they offer with great vigor: "NO!"

"Well, what about all of you?" I ask, changing the focus of their attention. "You all have eyes. Can you see?"

"YES!" comes the loud affirmative chorus.

"And you have ears. Can you hear?"

"YES!" they answer with greater volume.

"And you have noses. Can you smell?"

"YES!" This time their answer is mixed with numerous giggles.

"And it's obvious that you not only have mouths, but you can talk — because you keep answering my questions. So, what is the difference between you and this wooden cow?"

"We're alive!" Patrick responds with assurance.

"Oh! So you are," I agree, "and this wooden cow is not. Do you think God made this cow?"

"No," several children answer.

"Well then, who did?"

"A person," John replies.

"Yes," I continue, "a person did make it. And that's why there is such a big difference between it and all of you. Because GOD made you, AND gave you life. Only God can create and give life.

"The problem with idols is they are not alive. They cannot hear us or see us or touch us or understand us or love us. But God, the creator and giver of life, is very much able to do all of those things — and does.

"It is the spirit God has placed within you that makes you alive. It is the spirit within you that makes it possible for you to have relationships with other people and with God. You can't have a relationship with an idol like this cow because it has no spirit with which to respond to yours.

"Sometimes, when we are afraid, we will do really silly things. That's what the Israelites did in the wilderness when they made and worshiped the golden calf. They put their trust in an idol that could not possibly help them in their need because it wasn't alive, it had no spirit.

"To keep us from doing that, God gave us the second commandment — so we will remember to put our trust, our faith, where it belongs — in God. God made us, and only God deserves our deepest devotion, our worship, our trusting faith."

Serving Our Purpose

"And all of us, with unveiled faces, seeing the glory of the Lord as though reflected in a mirror, are being transformed into the same image from one degree of glory to another; for this comes from the Lord, the Spirit." — 2 Corinthians 3:18

Theme: *Change; the church; being ourselves; discipleship.*

Visual Aid: *A tablet, a sharpened pencil, and an unsharpened pencil.*

As the children settle onto the chancel steps and surrounding floor space, I hold up a tablet and a pencil, careful to conceal the point end of the pencil in my hand.

"What are these things for?" I ask.

"To write with," the children answer.

"So, what you're saying is, they have a purpose."

The children nod their agreement. Then I hand the tablet to one of the closer children and hold out the pencil to him, eraser end first. "Would you take this pencil and write your name for me?" I ask.

Mark grins and says, "Sure!" as he reaches for the pencil. His head goes down in concentration, he starts to write, then suddenly he jerks his attention from the tablet to me with an accusatory, "Funny!"

"What's wrong, Mark?" I ask with mock innocence.

"You need to sharpen this! It doesn't have a point," he complains.

"Would this one work better?" I ask reaching into my sleeve and producing a freshly sharpened pencil.

"Yeah!" he sort of growls. "You still want me to write my name?"

"Yes, please," I reply. "That was rather a dirty trick, wasn't it, Mark?"

His grin returns as he agrees that it was.

"Well, I didn't do that to be mean," I assure him. "I did it to make a point. You see, we all recognized that the purpose of the pencil was writing. But I wanted you to understand that it needed something more than just its purpose. It also needed to be prepared to fulfill that purpose. It had to be sharpened before it could be used to create a message or write a name. It had to be significantly changed in order to do what it was meant to do.

"I think the church in today's world is rather like this unsharpened pencil. It has a purpose, but because society and culture have changed a lot, the church is finding it more and more difficult to fulfill that purpose. Like the pencil, the church may have to undergo some change in order for the world to receive its message. It may need to consider offering alternative styles of worship or additional worship opportunities for folks at new times or even other days of the week. The church may have to be willing to try new things, stepping out of its traditional ways of being, in order to deliver the gospel message.

"People are like that too. God created each of us for a reason. All of us have a purpose. Sometimes we have to be willing to change in order to be who God created us to be. We may need to let go of anger or some prejudiced attitude that stands between ourselves and others. We may need to be brave enough to step outside of traditional, comfortable ways of being in order to be true disciples."

Prayer: "God, thank you for these young people with whom we are privileged to share and hear your message. Grant us the courage to make whatever changes we must in order to deliver that message to a world which is hungry to hear it. Let us go forth from this place with the love of Jesus in our hearts, that by that love, the world may know we are Christians. It is in the name of Jesus, our Lord and Savior, that we pray. Amen."

Spare Change

"You shall not steal."   — Exodus 20:15

Theme: *Honesty; discipleship; integrity.*

Visual Aid: *Two quarters and a nickel.*

"How many of you know there is a soda machine downstairs?" I begin. Virtually every one of the assembled children raises a hand.

"Oh, good!" I continue. "Since all of you know the church has a soda machine, you probably also all know how much a soda costs."

"Fifty cents!" comes their unified response.

"That's right," I agree. "And already this morning, I have been downstairs to buy a soda. I put one dollar into the machine. If a soda costs fifty cents, how much change do you think I got back?"

"Fifty cents!" they answer again.

"Well, that's what I expected to get back," I continue. "But, in addition to two quarters, I also got a nickel! I got fifty-FIVE cents in change." I hold up the two quarters and the nickel as I speak.

"I don't know why I got the nickel. I don't know if someone else had received it as change and just forgot to pick it up or if the machine somehow got confused and gave me back more than I should get. But however it happened, what I need to know is this: Is the nickel mine?"

Several children shake their heads negatively. Others say, "No."

"Well, I wonder to whom it belongs?"

"The soda company," Mary announces.

"The church?" Albert questions almost simultaneously.

"Yes," I affirm, "it probably does belong either to the company that fills the machine or to the church, which pays the company to

226

fill the machine. I think, since the church pays for the soda in the machine, the nickel probably belongs to the church.

"That being the case, if I keep the nickel, will I be stealing?"

Some of the younger children look doubtful, but several of the older ones nod affirmatively.

"We've been talking about the Ten Commandments for several weeks now, as you know. Today our pastor will be talking about the commandment that says, 'Don't steal.'

"Usually, when we think of stealing, we think about someone taking something that isn't his or hers on purpose. I did not mean to receive this extra nickel. I didn't decide to take something from the church or the soda company that wasn't mine. But even so, if I keep it, I think I would be stealing — because I know it belongs to someone else. That being the case, what do you think I should do with the nickel?"

"Put it back in the machine," David suggests.

"That would be one solution," I agree. "However, if I do, the next person will get it back in change. Then that person would have the same problem I have now."

"You need to put it in the offering tray," Sally tells me.

"I think you're right," I answer. "Does anyone know why I need to do that?"

"Because it belongs to the church."

"Because it isn't yours."

"Yes," I agree. "And there is one more reason. You see, if I hadn't mentioned what happened this morning, none of you would ever have known I had gotten a nickel that wasn't mine. No one would have known, except me ... and God. And God said, 'Don't steal.' Now, I value my relationship with God. And because I do, even if I hadn't told all of you about the spare change I got back this morning, I wouldn't have kept it. Because keeping it would mean I had to break one of God's commandments, one of the rules God gave to help me live my life. Doing that would disappoint God. Because I love God, I try to live as God would have me live. That's how it is with friends, with folks you care about and who care about you. You try not to have to disappoint them."

Prayer: "God, thank you for the lesson of the spare change this morning and for the commandments you have given us to help us live. Grant us the courage to keep them with love, following the example set for us by your son, Jesus Christ, our Lord and Savior, in whose name we pray. Amen."

Cutting Teeth

"But speaking the truth in love, we must grow up in every way to him who is the head, into Christ, from whom the whole body, joined and knit together by every ligament with which it is equipped, as each part is working properly, promotes the body's growth in building itself up in love." — Ephesians 4:15-16

Theme: *Community; working together; discipleship.*

Visual Aid: *A beaver puppet.*

"Good morning, everyone. I've brought a guest this morning to help us with our discussion." As I speak, I hold up the puppet beaver so all the children can see. "His name is 'Buckley,' and he's obviously some sort of animal. Does anyone know what kind of animal he is?"

"He's a beaver!" Tommy volunteers.

"Yes," I agree, "Buckley is a beaver. How did you know that, Tommy?"

"Because his tail is flat and he has buck teeth," Tommy replies.

"Well," I ask the group at large, "what do we know about beavers?"

"They build dams ..."

"They make their homes in the rivers ..."

"... and ponds too!"

"They cut down trees ..."

"They work very hard ..."

"My goodness," I respond, "you DO know a lot about beavers! And they do work very hard to build their homes in the water. They have to cut trees down — with their teeth! Is that how you would cut a tree down?"

"Of course not!" several children answer, giggling.

"I'd use a saw ..."

"I'd use an ax ..."

"Yes, a person would use tools to cut down a tree," I continue. "But beavers, like Buckley here, use the cutting tools they were born with — their teeth. It seems to me it would be *very* tiring to cut down a tree with your teeth — even if you had teeth that were made for the job. Then imagine the work involved in trimming off the branches, nudging the tree into the water, and getting it into just the right position to be a part of your house! What a LOT of work that would be — HARD work!

"Well, I brought all this up because there are some folks in our congregation who have been doing a lot of hard work too. They haven't been cutting down trees with their teeth, of course (more giggles erupt), but they have been taking surveys of the congregation and working on something called 'long-range planning.' That is, they've been trying to make plans for the future of our church, to help us identify things that may encourage church growth and to help us look at our resources so that we can plan for what we will need someday. They've also been looking at the way we use our resources now to try to decide if we need to make some changes in order to really be the church God wants us to be.

"You know, when a beaver like Buckley here builds a dam in a river, he doesn't do it all by himself. He lives with other beavers and they all build their house together.

230

"In a way, our congregation is like a colony of beavers. We must all work together in order to build up the church and plan for our future. If the members of the long-range planning committee had to do all the work by themselves, it would be about as impossible as it would be for Buckley to try to build a beaver dam by himself. But Buckley can depend on the other beavers to help him, can't you, Buckley?" As I ask this question, I make the puppet nod affirmatively. "And the long-range planning committee will be depending on everyone here to help them. They may ask for help with planning and making decisions; they may ask *you* folks to pray for them and the church. Whatever they need help with, it's important that we give them all the help we are able to give. That's part of what it means to live in a community built on love."

When Hope Is Gone

"Soon afterwards he went to a town called Nain, and his disciples and a large crowd went with him. As he approached the gate of the town, a man who had died was being carried out. He was his mother's only son, and she was a widow; and with her was a large crowd from the town. When the Lord saw her, he had compassion for her and said to her, 'Do not weep.' Then he came forward and touched the bier, and the bearers stood still. And he said, 'Young man, I say to you, rise!' The dead man sat up and began to speak, and Jesus gave him to his mother."

— Luke 7:11-15

Theme: *Hope; compassion.*

Visual Aid: *A toy spider.*

The spider I have brought for the children's sermon is actually a cat toy — eight bright red pipe cleaner legs, a black "body" of fake fur, and two little plastic eyes. As spiders go, it is very non-threatening.

Kneeling in front of the assembled children, I plop the spider down on the floor between us and ask, "What is this thing?"

"A spider!" most of them answer.

"What kind of a spider might it be?" I continue.

"A tarantula!" two of the boys assure me. Certainly it is about the size of a tarantula.

"It could be a tarantula," I agree. "But what other kind of spider could it be?"

"A wolf spider," Rebecca suggests.

"A garden spider," says Tommy.

"A black spider," Joe offers.

232

"Those are all good possibilities," I tell them. "But I'd like to explore the one Joe suggested — the black spider. Besides the tarantula, do any of you know of any other spiders that are black?" After a moment of silence, it becomes obvious that I have exhausted their repertoire of spider types.

"Have any of you ever heard of a black widow spider?" I question.

"Oh, yeah!" says Joe.

"Well," I continue, "since this is just a toy spider, I can have it be whatever type of spider I want it to be. And I thought of the black widow because I wanted to ask you why it's called a widow. Does anyone know what a widow is?"

Just when I think I've gotten into something too foreign to their experience, Marcia speaks up. "Isn't a widow someone whose husband is dead?"

"Yes, Marcia," I respond with relief. "A widow is someone whose husband has died. And the black widow spider gets her name because she tends to outlive her spider husband."[1]

"Now, I have another question. Does anyone know what 'only' means?" This draws puzzled looks so I ask, "What if you had *only* one toy? What would that mean?"

"That I didn't have to share it with anyone else," Richard announces with satisfied certainty.

It is difficult for me not to laugh as I affirm his response, saying, "Yes, it *could* mean you don't have to share it ..."

"It means I don't have any other toys, if it's my only toy," Jennifer interrupts.

"That's right, Jennifer," I answer. "Now, if this were your only toy, and I took it away from you, how would you feel?"

"Very sad," Jennifer replies.

"I'd be angry," Justin mutters.

"Probably you'd feel both sad and angry," I suggest. "And the reason I brought up these two words, 'widow' and 'only,' was to help us understand today's scripture. It is a story about a widow — someone whose husband had died. She lived in a town called Nain.

233

"Now, in the first century, women did not usually have jobs. They had to depend on their husbands and sons to provide money for food, clothing, and shelter. Since this woman was a widow, she had to depend on her *only* son. That is, she had just one son.

"As the story goes, this widow was in a very bad situation because her only son had just died! Her husband was already dead. And now her only son was dead too. Life must have looked pretty hopeless for her. Even in the midst of her grief for her son, she must have wondered who was going to take care of her now. She must have felt very sad. And she may have felt a bit angry too. It must have seemed like everything that mattered to her was over.

"She was walking along the road outside of Nain, behind her son's body which some men were carrying on a platform. They were going to bury him. But as they were walking to the cemetery, they met Jesus and the disciples coming the other way.

"Jesus immediately understood the situation. And he had such deep compassion for this widow that he told her, 'Do not weep.' Then he went over to the platform on which her son's body lay and said, 'Young man, arise!' And the boy did! And Jesus gave him back to his mother.

"I think there is something very important for us to learn from this story. It is a story about a widow for whom everything seemed lost. Then Jesus came along and gave her son back to her. He gave her son's life back — and he gave her life back too, because she depended on her son for food, and clothing, and all the basic things we need in life.

"There will be times in all of our lives when it will seem like everything is lost. There will be times when it seems like all hope for our future is gone. When those times come, it will be important to remember this story of the widow of Nain — to understand that just as Jesus met her on the road and restored her future, Jesus can come into our lives too and give us hope for life where we thought there was none."

Prayer: "God, thank you for the gift of *your* only son, Jesus, whom you sent to all of us in this world. Help us to understand, as we walk the roads of our lives, that you are there with us, that you send Jesus to meet us, that you restore life to us through your beloved son, in whose name we pray. Amen."

---

1. This understatement of circumstance brings a roar of laughter from the congregation at large, which I ignore. There are boundaries beyond which one must not tread with children, lest their theology be confused. When I decided to use the spider to get to today's point, I knew I had better not tell them that black widows ate their mates, or they might conclude the widow of Nain had devoured her spouse.

The Guy In The Ditch

" 'Which of these three, do you think, was a neighbor to the man who fell into the hands of the robbers?' He said, 'The one who showed him mercy.' Jesus said to him, 'Go and do likewise.' "   — Luke 10:36-37

Theme: Love; mercy; kindness; neighborliness.

Visual Aid: A highway map, several published trail guides, and a Bible.

After the children gather, I hold up the highway map which I have partially unfolded. "What is this?" I ask. Everyone agrees it is a map.

"What are some reasons we might use a map?" I continue.

"To find out how to get someplace," Mary suggests.

"To find the best way to go," Charles adds.

"Yes," I answer, "we can use maps for both of those things. In addition, the little symbols on the map tell us some of the points of interest we might want to see along the way."

Next I hold up the guides to various area trails, but they are not as easy as the map for the children to identify. Noting the interested, but puzzled, looks on the children's faces, I tell them, "These are guides to some of our local trails. Like the map, they give us information about places to go, how to get there, and what there is to do along the way."

Next I hold up the Bible. "What is this?" I ask.

"The Bible!" comes the children's unhesitating response.

"Yes, it's the Bible," I agree. "And, like the map and trail guides, this is a guide too. It also tells us where to go, how to get there, and what there is to do along the way. It's full of stories, and one of those stories is about some men who were traveling from

Jerusalem to Jericho. Have any of you ever heard of the Good Samaritan?"

About half the children indicate they have. "Okay," I continue. "This is a story some of you already know. It begins with a man who was walking down the road to Jericho. As he walked along, he was attacked by some robbers who beat him up! They stole everything the man had, even his *clothes*! Then they left him, naked and bleeding, in the ditch by the side of the road.

"Pretty soon, a priest came along. He saw the guy in the ditch, but he carefully avoided him, passing by on the far side of the road. Next a Levite came along. He also saw the bleeding man lying in the ditch, and, like the priest, the Levite avoided the guy and passed on.

"Now, in their defense, I have to say that the priest and the Levite were only doing what they thought was right. In their culture, a person who was bleeding was considered unclean. It would have been a very serious thing for either of them to have touched the guy in the ditch — and they would have had to touch him in order to help him. So, they weren't just being mean by passing on. They were avoiding all of the inconvenience of days and days of ceremonial cleansing they would have to go through if they touched the wounded man. But, they were also thinking more of their own needs than of the needs of the person in the ditch.

"However, a third person came by. He was a Samaritan. He had more reason that the first two men to avoid the guy in the ditch. Not only was the wounded man bleeding (and therefore unclean), he was also a Jew. And, you see, the Jews and the Samaritans had been enemies for a very long time because of some religious differences. Under normal circumstances, Samaritans and Jews would not even speak to each other.

"And yet, it was the Samaritan who stopped to help the wounded man. The Samaritan helped him up, bound up his wounds, put the battered man on his own animal, and took him to a nearby inn. There the Samaritan paid the innkeeper to take care of the Jew. The Samaritan even told the innkeeper, 'If you spend more money to take care of him than I have given you, I will pay you the difference when I return.'

"What do you think would have happened to the man in the ditch if the Samaritan had followed the rules of his culture like the first two men did?"

"He might have died," Charles answers.

"That's right," I agree. "And yet the Samaritan, whom the Jew himself would have considered an enemy, took care of this total stranger. What a big heart the Samaritan must have had, to care for someone else like that — someone he didn't even know!"

"This story tells us some very important things. It tells us that everyone, no matter how poor, how beaten, or how dirty he might be — everyone is our neighbor. And it tells us that God's rules aren't the same as human rules.

"You know, we have many roadmaps in our lives — guides that tell us where to go, and how to stay on the path. But this story tells us that sometimes it's important to have enough courage to step off the path, to step outside the rules we know, if following the rules would make us act unkindly to another person.

"Jesus acted outside the rules all the time. He healed people on the Sabbath. He ate dinner with people other folks thought were dirty and unworthy of good company. But Jesus never saw anyone as unworthy. And he gave us a different set of rules by which to live, rules of love, mercy, and kindness. Jesus taught us to love our neighbors as ourselves."

Prayer: "God, thank you for your Son, Jesus, who told these wonderful stories so long ago, stories which continue to show us the way to follow him. When we come to those times in our lives when we have to choose between the rules and kindness, help us, O God, to be kind. Help us to be good neighbors to everyone we meet along the way. Amen."

A Feast Of Love

"You prepare a table before me in the presence of my enemies ..."   — Psalm 23:5

Theme: *Love; communion; reconciliation.*

Visual Aid: *A checkered dish towel or small tablecloth and a heart cut out of wood.*

After greeting the children, I ask, "What does it mean to have an enemy?"

"It means there's someone who doesn't like you," Carla answers.

"That's right ... and it could also mean someone you don't like," I respond.

"We've been going through Psalm 23 for several weeks, and today we've come to the fifth verse. It begins, 'You prepare a table before me in the presence of my enemies ...' That's why I asked what it means to have an enemy. It's fairly common when someone doesn't like us for us not to like them either. And if someone dislikes us enough to pick a fight, it's pretty normal to feel like fighting back. Since we're talking about this, I'd like all of you to make a fist." I demonstrate by making a fist of my own.

"Now, while you hold those fists, I want you to tell me who it is that prepares a table for us?"

"God?" John questions.

"Yes, John. God prepares the table ..." As I speak, I unfold a checkered cloth and spread it on the floor in front of the children. "... and God sets that table with love." With these words I place a heart (cut from wood and painted red) in the center of the cloth.

"And you know, a really interesting part of this verse says that God prepares this table in the presence of our enemies. So, that's got to mean that if I have an enemy and God invites me to this

239

table, God's probably going to invite my enemy too — because, even though I may not like that person, God loves that person just as much as me! Wow!"

"While you think about that for a moment I need a couple of you, *without opening your fists*, to try to pick up this heart ..."

Several children immediately pounce. They quickly realize they cannot pick it up with their fists closed. But two of them start pushing on opposite sides of the heart, and manage to pick it up together.

"Aha! George and Donna managed to do it — but only by working together. Let's think about that for a moment ... I wonder, would you two have helped each other if you were enemies?"

"Probably not," George answers.

"So," I ask all the children, "if George had an enemy and both George and his enemy were invited to this feast of love, what would they have to do in order to participate in the feast?"

"They'd have to open their fists and let go of their anger with each other," Matt answers. "Otherwise, they'd go away without any love," he continues. And once again I am blessed by the wisdom of a young theologian.

"That's right, Matt. In order to receive love," I suggest as I pick up the heart, "and in order to give love," I continue as I hand the heart to the child beside me, indicating she should pass it on

around, "we have to open our fists; we have to let go of our anger; we have to be open to one another and love one another, even our enemies, in order to receive the love God freely offers."

Prayer: "Dear God, we thank you for the feast of love you place before us in every moment of our lives. We thank you for your son Jesus who came to show us how to live together, teaching us to love one another. Help us to have the courage to follow his example, loving everyone, even those who do not love us. In Jesus' name we pray. Amen."

Where Does God Live?

"The God who made the world and everything in it, he who is Lord of heaven and earth, does not live in shrines made by human hands ... From one ancestor he made all nations to inhabit the whole earth, and he allotted the times of their existence and the boundaries of the places where they would live, so that they would search for God and perhaps grope for him and find him — though indeed he is not far from each one of us. For 'in him we live and move and have our being'; as even some of your own poets have said, 'For we too are his offspring.'" — Acts 17:24, 26-28

Theme: *Community; relationships; God's presence; love.*

Visual Aid: *A 3-foot x 5-foot (i.e., large) world map and a passport.*

As the children seat themselves on the chancel steps, I spread out a map of the world on the floor in front of them.

"Ooooooooooooooooh!" comes their response as the map's features are revealed.

"It's pretty!" Mary exclaims.

"Yes, it is pretty, Mary," I answer. "There are lots of different colors to help us see where all the different countries are. Can any of you show us where we live?"

Immediately some of the eight- and nine-year-olds spring from their seats and descend on the map like bees on a field of clover. Almost with one motion, five little index fingers land in the center of the United States.

"Right HERE!" Thomas announces. I am duly impressed by the children's knowledge of geography.

"You all certainly know where Missouri is," I affirm. "Thank you." As the children return to their seats, I continue, pointing to the corresponding places on the map: "What if I wanted to go from the United States over to China? Could I just get on a plane and

242

go, or would I need to take something along that would give me permission to enter a foreign country?"

"You'd have to take money," Sarah replies.

"Well, that's true, Sarah," I answer as visions of bribing border guards flit through my thoughts. "Money would certainly make my trip easier. But is there anything else I'd have to take along?"

"You'd need a passport," Jane says matter-of-factly.

"Ah, yes. I'd need a passport," I echo. "If I went to China, I would have to cross borders of other countries, nations that have laws and governments that are different from ours, I would need something called a 'passport' that would give me permission to enter those other countries. In fact, I've brought my passport this morning so you can see what one looks like. It's a little book with my picture in it and pages for government officials to use a rubber stamp to show it's all right for me to come into their countries." As I speak, I show the children these parts of the passport; then I give it to the nearest child to hand around the group.

"Do any of you know who made the laws in these countries? Who decided where the borders should be? Who made all these barriers between nations?"

"People did," James answers.

"That's right, James. But who made the world?"

"God!" he tells me.

"Right again. So, what I'm wondering now is, can any of you show me where in the world God lives?"

"HERE!" Ricky announces, planting his finger in the middle of the Atlantic Ocean.

With a barely suppressed chuckle, I answer, "Indeed God does live there, Ricky. And here ... and here ... and here ..." Each time I say "here," I point to a different spot on the map. "And if God lives every place in the world, does God need a passport?"

"No!" the children answer together.

"No," I continue, "God doesn't need a passport. People do, because of all the rules, laws, borders, and barriers we have set up. But God doesn't. In fact, God sent Jesus to us to break down all the barriers we put between ourselves and other people because

God really cares about relationships. God cares about being present to us and about our being present to God and to each other.

"We decided a moment ago that God lives everywhere in the world. And that means that God lives in you ... and you ... and you ... and me." Once again, as I say these words, I point to different children and then to myself. "God lives in the smile of a friend, in the hug you give to someone else, in the hands we use to help one another, and in the kind things we do each day. God lives in every one of us and in every person throughout the world.

"We are all God's children, no matter what country we live in, no matter what street we live on, no matter what church we may or may not attend. We are God's children and God wants us to live together in this world as brothers and sisters, loving one another, just as God loves us."

The Better Part

"Now as they went on their way, he entered a certain village, where a woman named Martha welcomed him into her home. She had a sister named Mary, who sat at the Lord's feet and listened to what he was saying. But Martha was distracted by her many tasks; so she came to him and asked, 'Lord, do you not care that my sister has left me to do all the work by myself? Tell her then to help me.' But the Lord answered her, 'Martha, Martha, you are worried and distracted by many things; there is need of only one thing. Mary has chosen the better part, which will not be taken away from her.' " — Luke 10:38-42

Theme: *Stress; making choices; helping one another.*

Visual Aid: *A basket suspended by its handle from a strong rubber band; a work glove; a small bag of toys such as marbles, a doll, and a stuffed animal; a mathematics textbook; a music book; a baseball; a can of pet food; a Bible; a box to hold all this stuff.*

As the children come to the front of the sanctuary, I take the work glove and basket out of the box and ask one of the taller boys if he will help me out this morning. He agrees, so I hand him the glove and ask him to put it on. Then I hand him the basket with instructions to hold it up by hanging onto the rubber band attached to the handle.

By now the rest of the children have become quite intrigued. Addressing the young man holding the basket, I say, "Adam, we're going to put some things into the basket. I don't *think* the rubber band will break (Adam's eyes grow wide with surprise and a hint of distress at my words), but just in case it does, that's why I asked you to wear the glove. It will protect your hand from being hurt if the rubber band snaps." Relief washes over Adam's face as giggles ripple through the assembled children and congregation.

245

Turning to the rest of the children, I ask, "What are some of the things that take up your time?"

"School!" Mary volunteers.

"It does take a lot of time, doesn't it, Mary," I agree as I pull the mathematics book out of the box. "In fact, you not only go to school five days a week, you have homework too, don't you?"

Mary nods affirmatively as I place the textbook in the basket, causing the rubber band to stretch and Adam to don a wary look.

"What else takes your time?" I continue.

"Soccer! Football! Basketball!" come several replies at once.

"Ah, so sports are a big factor for some of you. All right, I've brought a baseball to represent sports." I take the baseball out of the box and put it in the basket. "What else takes your time?"

"Cleaning up my room," Joe offers with a groan.

"Well, let's see ..." I pause peering into the box. "I suppose that includes picking up and putting away your toys, so we can use this bag with marbles and such to represent cleaning up your room." I have intentionally chosen heavy toys, and as I place the bag of toys into the basket, it sinks toward the floor — but the rubber band does not snap.

"Are there other things that take your time?" I continue.

"Piano lessons," Kristopher answers, "and practice," he adds, almost as an afterthought.

"Yes, learning the piano or any other musical instrument takes many hours of practice," I agree. "We can put this music book in the basket to represent music lessons."

"What about animals?" I inquire. "Do any of you have pets you have to feed?"

"Yeah, and it's my turn to feed the dog this week," Rachel offers with a sigh.

"And that takes time, right?" I ask her. She nods agreement. "So, we can put this can of pet food in to represent the time we take to care for our animals," I suggest, as my actions follow my words.

"This basket is getting quite full, isn't it?" I ask the children. They agree.

"And it's getting heavy, too!" Adam offers.

"Yes, I suspect it is, Adam. Let me help you hold it up," I offer, putting my hand beneath the basket itself, and taking some of the weight off the rubber band. "Now," I continue, "there is at least one more thing that takes some of our time — at least I hope it does ..."

"Oh yes!" Tim exclaims. "Church!"

"That's right, Tim. I hope you spend some of your time every week coming to church and Sunday School. I hope you spend a lot of your time with God, whether it's here in worship, or studying in your classes, reading your Bibles, praying, or just sort of hanging out with God. I've brought this Bible to represent that part of our lives, only our basket is so full, I'm not sure it will fit."

Precariously I balance the Bible on the other items in the basket where it remains for just a moment, then slides off. "Oops! The basket is too full. Adam, if this basket represented your life you'd find it hard to fit anything else in, wouldn't you?"

Adam nods wearily.

"You may put the basket down now," I tell him, helping him to ease it to the floor. "I really appreciate your help with this," I continue.

Then turning to the group at large, I ask, "What happened when we tried to include the Bible in our basket of stuff?"

"It slid off," the children answer.

"Why did that happen, Jennifer?"

"Because the basket was too full of other stuff," she answers.

"That's right, Jennifer. And sometimes I think our lives are a lot like that basket. We get them so filled with things that keep us busy, we don't have time for church, for prayer, for our relationship with God. And when our lives get that full, we suffer in another way too. We start to feel what we call stress or tension. That's sort of like what you saw happening to the rubber band. The more we put in the basket, the more tension and stress there was on the rubber band. If we could have put even more things in the basket, what would have happened eventually?"

"The rubber band would have broken," Wesley announces.

"That's right. And life can be like that too. When we get too busy, when our lives get too filled up with activities and we don't

247

have room for anything else, much less time for our relationships — with one another and with God — then we're in danger of snapping just like that rubber band.

"What happened when I pushed up on the bottom of the basket, Adam?"

"It was easier to hold on to," he answers.

"Well, I think that's another lesson we can learn from this demonstration: That it's easier to carry our load when we have help. That's part of what it means to be in a community such as the church. It means we don't have to carry our burdens alone. We have others to help us out.

"There's a story in the Gospel of Luke about two ladies who were sisters. Their names were Mary and Martha. Martha had a LOT of work to do — you might say her basket was much too full.

"Well, Jesus came to visit these two sisters, and Mary left her sister in the kitchen to do all the work while she sat in the living room listening to Jesus tell stories. Mary was making time for Jesus in her life; but if she had helped her sister with the chores in the kitchen, they might both have had more time to spend with Jesus.

"Sometimes it's hard to ask for help. Sometimes our lives get too busy and we don't even realize it until something really important comes along like it did for Mary and Martha when Jesus came to visit. Sometimes it's important to help others with their tasks — with the loads they have to carry — sharing our time to give them more time. You know, time is one of the greatest gifts we have to give one another."

Prayer: "God, thank you for giving us the freedom to make choices about our time and how we spend it. Help us to always make time for you in our lives. In the name of Jesus, our friend and savior, we pray. Amen."

Count On It!

"Now faith is the assurance of things hoped for, the conviction of things not seen."   — Hebrews 11:1

Theme: *Faith, trust, change.*

Visual Aid: *Several "fronds" from a walnut tree.*

Holding up the walnut leaves I've brought, I ask the assembled children, "Does anyone know what kind of tree these are from?"

"Eucalyptus," Jerry suggests with a broad grin. He's one of the older children. I recognize his desire to emphasize that fact with his use of a strange, big word.

"Now that's a clever guess," I respond. "In fact, I think the eucalyptus tree does have leaves similar to this; but these are not eucalyptus leaves."

"Pine!" Mike then offers. He's too young to know that pine trees have needles.

"That's a good guess, Michael, but these leaves aren't from a pine tree either. Actually, they came off a walnut tree. An interesting thing about the walnut tree is that it is the last tree to get its leaves in the spring and the first one to lose them in the fall. Has anyone noticed anything special about these leaves?"

"Some of them are yellow," Amanda announces.

"That's right," I agree. "Some are still green, but some of them have turned yellow. After they change color, what will happen next?"

"They'll fall off," Dylan replies.

"So you're telling me that after a period of time all the leaves will fall off the tree?" I question. Dylan nods agreement.

"Let's look at these leaves a little more closely for a moment," I suggest. "Can everyone see the holes?" I hold the leaves up so that light makes the holes more evident. "It looks like insects have been making quite a meal off these leaves, doesn't it? And the edges of some of the leaves have been tattered and torn by the wind. These leaves look a bit worn out — kind of like a favorite pair of jeans that you wear a lot. When you wear your clothes out, what do you do?"

"Go get new ones," several young voices answer at once.

"So, what's the walnut tree going to do since its leaves are wearing out?"

"Get new ones?" Becky asks.

"Yes, after passing through the winter, the tree will get new leaves in the spring. But, if it didn't let go of the old leaves, there would be no room for the new ones. Now, as far as I know, trees don't think. But if they did ... If trees actually KNEW that they were going to have to let go of their leaves in the fall and stand bare-branched against the cold of winter, *trusting* that they would get new leaves in the spring, don't you think that might be a little scary?

"You know, we face changes in our lives every day, and sometimes change is scary for us because we don't know what will happen; we don't know what to expect. How many of you are going to go to school on Tuesday?" Many hands go up in reply.

"Are any of you going to school for the very first time?" I continue. Two children raise their hands.

"Wow! That's a *big* change for you!" I note. "And, the rest of you who are going back to school, I suppose you're going to return to the same grade as last year?"

"Of course not!" Mike snickers.

"Well, what if you did go back to the same class? What if you never changed grades?" I ask.

"You'd never grow up," Melinda wisely observes.

"Ahhhh ... So we *must* make changes in our lives in order to grow up. You're right, Melinda. Sometimes the changes life brings are small. Sometimes they're big — like changing schools, getting a new brother or sister, moving to a new city. Whether the changes are big or small, we have to trust that they will work out for the best. One way we get the courage to trust is knowing that there is something which *never* changes, no matter what: God's

251

love for us. No matter what changes life brings, you can always count on God's love.

"God set the sun and moon and stars in motion. God set the earth turning which causes the changing seasons. God made trees to grow and change with those seasons. God made each of you to grow and change too. God has something very special in mind for every one of you. So, whatever changes life brings, remember God is with you through them. You can count on it!"

Turned On

"For Christ did not send me to baptize but to proclaim the gospel, and not with eloquent wisdom, so that the cross of Christ might not be emptied of its power. For the message about the cross is foolishness to those who are perishing, but to us who are being saved it is the power of God." — 1 Corinthians 1:17-18

Theme: *Grace, love, friendship, Divine power, light.*

Visual Aid: *An extension cord and a small lamp.*

As the children gather I set a lamp on the floor and begin untangling an extension cord which I have previously determined is long enough to reach from the chancel steps to the outlet in the front of the sanctuary. Then I welcome the children and ask, "What do I need to do to get this lamp to work?"

"Plug it in," several children assert as one voice.

"Okay, then ... Let's see, we need a power source ..." I begin to look around as if to find an outlet.

"There's a plug over there!" Jennifer announces, pointing it out.

"Ah, so there is. Matt, would you take this cord and plug it in over there, please?" I've chosen Matt both because he is one of the older children and because he is on the side of the group closest to the outlet.

As Matt is carrying out his task, I ask the other children, "Why is Matt plugging the cord into the wall?"

"To get electricity," is offered simultaneously with, "To get power."

"So, you're telling me this lamp needs a power source in order to provide light?" I question. The children nod affirmatively.

Once Matt has the cord plugged into the outlet, I connect the cord to the lamp. Then I look at the children, mystified. "Well, gee," I puzzle, "the lamp still is not lighted. We have it plugged in ..."

"You have to turn it on," Terry notes with a hint of exasperation at my obvious lack of electrical expertise. As if to underline his opinion of my prowess, he reaches for the switch and turns on the light.

"Thank you, Terry," I continue, suggesting with a gentle shake of my head that he NOT shine the lamp in the faces of his companions. "What you've shown us is that just having a source of power is not enough; we also have to turn the switch on so the lamp can receive the power, right?"

From the top row, Bobby says in a big voice, "Well, yeah. You HAVE to turn it on to get the light."

"That's right, Bobby," I agree, "and I wonder if this lamp and its switch can tell us something about life. Who provides power in our lives?"

The wait time is long enough that I begin to get edgy before Katherine says, "God."

"Yes," I respond, "God created us; because of God, we live. All the power of our lives comes from God. But in addition to life, God gave us free will. That means we are free to make choices about how we live.

"Now God wants us to live with love and joy. And because God cares so much about how we live, God sent Jesus to us — the most precious gift imaginable: God's only son. Jesus came to show us how to live with one another and how to connect to God; Jesus came to empower our lives.

"Marcia," I turn to the youngster right in front of me, "suppose I wanted to give you a gift, but you just sat there with your arms folded. Would you be able to receive my gift?"

"No," she answers. "I'd have to open my arms."

"Yep," I agree. "So, I can't give you something if you are not willing to receive it. That is the case with any gift, including the gifts God would give us. Just like the lamp needed to be turned on in order to receive the electrical power, we need to open our arms, open our hearts, open ourselves to receive God and the power God offers for the living of our lives. We need to be 'turned on' to God.

"What are some of the ways in which we can receive God into our lives?" I ask, knowing questions are a risky business.

"First we have to get plugged in," Matt says with a grin.

"Ah ... okay, Matt. Would you like to explain that a little more?" I knew he was grinning because he knew he had me; he was old enough to enjoy mind games.

"Well, sure," Matt responds, "We have to get plugged in. You know, connected. That's why we come to church."

And so it is. "That's very good, Matt," I reply, broadening his grin with my obvious relief.

"So, what are some other ways in which we get turned on to God?" I ask.

"Through prayer?" Janice offers.

"Yes, definitely through prayer," I answer. "We also connect with God in other ways. We connect with God whenever we follow the example Jesus gave us for the living of our lives. We

connect with God when we receive the love God offers, by receiving Jesus into our lives. And, having made that connection, we bring the light of God's love to the world in the message of the story we know as the gospel — the message of the story about Jesus coming from God and loving us so much that he was even willing to die on a cross so that we might be reconnected with God. That's really powerful love.

"And that power, that love, is ours for all time. God offers it to us; but we have to do our part too. For not even God can give us what we are not willing to receive. The choice is ours. And when we choose to receive God's love, given to us in Jesus Christ, then we can live our lives turned on to God, carrying the light of God's love to all the world."

What's Inside

"God chose what is low and despised in the world, things that are not, to reduce to nothing things that are, so that no one might boast in the presence of God. He is the source of your life in Christ Jesus, who became for us wisdom from God, and righteousness and sanctification and redemption, in order that, as it is written, 'Let the one who boasts, boast in the Lord.'"

— 1 Corinthians 1:28-31

Theme: *Boasting; children of God; love; talents; thanksgiving.*

Visual Aid: *A paper dusk jacket from a hardbound novel slipped onto a Bible.*

This morning a large group of children has assembled, their numbers increased by junior-high youths who are visiting from another denomination. I begin by holding up the covered Bible, and ask one of the older children to read the title on the cover.

"*A Piece of the Moon Is Missing,*"[1] Arthur responds.

"My goodness," I answer, "*A Piece of the Moon Is Missing!*" Does that sound like an interesting story?"

"No," young John pipes up with a growl, little knowing he's actually helped me with his negative attitude.

"Well, if it sounds that bad, John, let's set it aside for a minute while I ask everyone about something else. Does anyone know what it means to boast?" Several of the older children grin, but everyone remains silent as I begin to wonder if this is going to be "one of THOSE days."

"If I were boasting," I rephrase my question, "what would I be doing?"

"Bragging," Rick answers.

"Ah, so boasting is bragging," I reply. "Well, then, I wonder if any of you have anything to boast about — anything to brag about."

257

"I have a cat and I bet you don't," John immediately responds in a sing-song voice, echoing his statement with a mocking, "Nyeh, nyeh, nyeh-nyeh, nyeh!"

"Ooooh, thank you, John," I compliment, refusing to be drawn into whatever has caused such sourpuss behavior. My thanks bring a glance of surprise as I continue: "You've not only got something to brag about, you've given us an example of your bragging! You're boasting that you have a cat and you bet I don't — and even if I do, it can't be as good as your cat, right?" This question brings a reluctant grin to John's face.

Returning my attention then to the whole group, I ask, "What are some of the reasons people brag?"

"Because they're proud of something," Marcia suggests.

"Because they think they're better than someone else," Harry answers.

"Yes, people sometimes brag for both of those reasons," I reply. "Sometimes people think they won't be accepted just as they are so they brag or boast about themselves hoping to make themselves more likable, or to make themselves seem better than someone else. That sort of boasting is like putting on a false front or a mask almost."

As I pronounce the last few words, I pick up the book John did not think sounded interesting and draw it again to the children's attention as I say, "In some ways boasting is like this book. It looks like a mystery novel with an interesting story. Actually ..." (I begin to take the slipcover off the Bible as I continue), "it's not one story but a whole collection of stories." Surprised recognition appears on many young faces as I reveal beneath the cover a very familiar book.

"It's the Bible," Susan exclaims.

"That's right, Susan. And you know, when I put the cover of a novel on it, not one word inside of the Bible changed. The cover didn't affect what's inside at all. And of course, it's what's on the inside that counts, not what's on the outside.

"When the Bible had the cover on it, it appeared to be something it was not. Just like sometimes when people boast — they appear to be something they really aren't — something that really

258

doesn't have anything at all to do with who they really are or with what is important about them.

"Now, the reason I've brought all of this up today is because of the scripture which was read right before you came up here. It was from one of Saint Paul's letters to the church at Corinth. Paul wrote to these folks and told them to quit arguing with one another — to quit boasting to each other about who had baptized them.

"You see, some of the Corinthians were saying, 'I was baptized by Apollo, and that is a LOT better than being baptized by anyone else.' Others were saying, 'I was baptized by Peter and you weren't.' Paul told them that it didn't matter who had baptized any of them; what mattered was the change that had taken place within them because of their baptism. What mattered was who they were as Christians — who they were on the inside.

"You know, the arguments among the Corinthians would be about like someone today boasting that he is a Methodist, and someone else bragging that she is a Baptist and that's better, and then a Presbyterian and a Christian Disciple both jumping into the argument claiming that they are better than either of the first two — NONE of which really matters. What matters is what's inside of them, hearts transformed by the love of Jesus Christ, and that no matter what denomination they might outwardly be a member of, ALL of them are Christians underneath their outer labels — on the inside.

"There are times in our lives when we may feel like bragging. There may be some special talent we have in sports, or music, or schoolwork that we'd really like to boast about. But it's important to remember that the talents we have are gifts from God. If we boast about them, we need to boast about the Giver rather than about ourselves.

"That's what Paul told the Corinthians too: 'Let the one who boasts, boast in the Lord' (1 Corinthians 1:31). When we boast about the Lord who has given us life and talents to share, then we don't have the attitude that we're better than someone else, because we realize that all of us are children of God, and each of us has special gifts to share.

259

"And you know, the things that seem so important that we are tempted to brag about them, usually don't make much difference at all. The boasting, the bragging is just a cover. It's what's inside of us that counts — love for God and for one another."

---

1. Johnson, James L., *A Piece of the Moon Is Missing* (New York: J. B. Lippincott Company, 1979).

Scriptural Index

Topical Index